THE GRAMMATICAL STRUCTURES OF

ENGLISH AND GERMAN

A CONTRASTIVE SKETCH

Herbert L. Kufner

THE UNIVERSITY OF CHICAGO PRESS

CHICAGO AND LONDON

This work was developed pursuant to a contract between
the United States Office of Education and the Center for Applied Linguistics
of the Modern Language Association, and is published with permission
of the United States Office of Education.

‡

International Standard Book Number: 0–226–45678–1

Library of Congress Catalog Card Number: 62–19625

The University of Chicago Press, Chicago 60637
The University of Chicago Press, Ltd., London

THE GRAMMATICAL STRUCTURES
OF ENGLISH AND GERMAN

CONTRASTIVE STRUCTURE SERIES

Charles A. Ferguson

General Editor

GENERAL INTRODUCTION
TO THE SERIES

This study is part of a series of contrastive structure studies which describe the similarities and differences between English and each of the five foreign languages most commonly taught in the United States: French, German, Italian, Russian, and Spanish. Each of the five languages is represented by two volumes in the series, one on the sound systems and the other on the grammatical systems of English and the language in question. The volumes on sounds make some claim to completeness within the limits appropriate to these studies; the volumes on grammar, however, treat only selected topics, since complete coverage would be beyond the scope of the series. The studies are intended to make available for the language teacher, textbook writer, or other interested reader a body of information which descriptive linguists have derived from their contrastive analyses of English and the other languages.

The Center for Applied Linguistics, in undertaking this series of studies, has acted on the conviction held by many linguists and specialists in language teaching that one of the major problems in the learning of a second language is the interference caused by the structural differences between the native language of the learner and the second language. A natural consequence of this conviction is the belief that a careful contrastive analysis of the two languages offers an excellent basis for the preparation of instructional materials, the planning of courses, and the development of actual classroom techniques.

The project got under way in the summer of 1959. The primary responsibility for the various parts of the project fell to specialists of demonstrated competence in linguistics having a strong interest in the application of linguistics to practical problems of language teaching. Wherever possible, a recognized senior scholar specializing in the foreign language was selected either as a consultant or as an author.

Since it did not seem likely that the users of the series would generally read all five studies, considerable duplication was permitted in the material presented. Also, although a general framework was suggested for the studies and some attempt was made to achieve a uniformity of procedure by consultation among those working on the project, each team was given free rein to follow its own approach. As a result, the parts of the series vary in style, terminology, notation, and in the relative emphasis given to different aspects of the analysis.

Some differences in these studies are also due to the wide range of variation in American English, especially in the pronunciation of vowels. No special consideration was given to English spoken outside America since the studies were primarily intended for language teachers and textbook writers in this country. There are also differences in the studies which depend on the structure of each of the foreign languages under comparison. Thus, if a fact of English agrees well with a feature of German it may merit little mention, if any, in an English-German contrastive study, but if the same fact differs in a complicated and highly significant way from a corresponding feature of Spanish, it may require elaborate treatment in an English-Spanish study.

In the course of the project several by-products were produced, two of which are worth noting as of possible interest to readers of volumes in this series. One, Linguistic Reading Lists for Teachers of Modern Languages (Washington, D.C., 1962) was compiled chiefly by linguists working on the project and contains a carefully selected and annotated list of works which linguists would recommend to the teacher of French, German, Italian, Russian, or Spanish. The other, W. W. Gage's Contrastive Studies in Linguistics (Washington, D.C., 1961) consists of an unannotated listing of all contrastive studies which had come to the attention of the Center by the summer of 1961.

Although the value of contrastive analysis has been recognized for some time, relatively few substantial studies have been published. In a sense, then, this series represents a pioneering venture in the field of applied linguistics and, as with all such ventures, some of the material may eventually turn out to be of little value and some of the methods used may turn out to be inadequate. The authors and editor are fully convinced of the value of the studies, however, and hope that the series will represent an important step in the application of linguistic procedures to language problems. They are also agreed in their expectation that, while in another ten years this series may seem primitive and unsatisfactory, the principles of contrastive analysis will be more widely recognized and appreciated.

Charles A. Ferguson
Director, Center for Applied Linguistics

PREFACE

This book is not intended as a structural description or as a grammar of German: it makes no claim of completeness or even uniqueness. Its purpose is rather to be maximally useful for American language teachers and writers of textbooks by dwelling on those areas where German and English are most different. Its major emphasis is on syntax, the traditional stepchild of grammatical studies. Very little space is devoted to morphological problems. The spoken language is stressed because I believe the teaching of German should proceed from the spoken language. Nevertheless, the written language and the problems which are peculiarly characteristic of written style have not been neglected.

I should like to express my indebtedness and gratitude to my former teacher Professor William G. Moulton, now at Princeton University. The imprint of his help and guidance can be found on every page of this study.

H.L.K.

TABLE OF CONTENTS

GERMAN SENTENCE TYPES

Before we look into the structure of German phrases and clauses, we shall attempt to define and classify the favorite sentence types of German.

There are two sentence definitions which are widely used in today's grammar books. The first one is notional and is perhaps best formulated by Otto Jespersen (Philosophy of Grammar, p. 307):

> A sentence is a (relatively) complete and independent human utterance—the completeness and independence of it being shown by its standing alone or its capability of standing alone, i.e., of being uttered by itself.

The other sentence definition which haunts the textbooks is a formal one:

> A sentence is a group of words containing a subject and a predicate, and it must not be subordinated to a larger construction so as to form a dependent clause.

This second definition we shall have to discard at the very outset since we all know that in both English and German there exist large numbers of utterances which we wish to call sentences and which do not contain a subject and a predicate. Leaving aside for the moment such complete utterances as Nein or Natürlich, there is a group of sentences in German which contains only a predicate: Mich friert or Hier wird sonntags getanzt.

The notional definition of Jespersen is worded in such a way as to include such utterances as Guten Morgen and Unsinn. Such utterances, as Jespersen and many other analysts point out, are fully as self-supporting and complete as sentences which do contain a subject and a predicate: Ich wünsche Ihnen einen guten Morgen or Das ist Unsinn.

This is, of course, true; yet it does not result in a definition which provides us with a useful tool by which we can separate sentences from non-sentences, unless we can say what we mean by completeness or even relative completeness. In a very real sense, very few groups of words which we would unanimously punctuate as sentences can really be called complete or capable of standing alone. Let us, for example, look at the utterance: Das hat er damit gemeint. We would all expect our students to capitalize the first word of this utterance and to put a period at the end. But in what sense is it really complete? Can it really stand alone? We should at least know the reference of das, damit, and er if we are to derive a meaning. Thus this sentence is not complete and self-supporting at all, but totally dependent on information given by antecedents outside this sentence. Everyone of us could produce innumerable sentences of this type which would have meaning only in connected discourse: like most of the sentences that we speak, they are dependent on what has been said before.

If we think of it in terms of teaching, this notional definition of a sentence shows its most serious weakness. It is, indeed, a completely subjective definition. A number of lexical items uttered in sequence is a sentence if it is complete. However, since there are no formal signs of completeness, we are left without means of explaining completeness to a student who does not already know. We are reduced to a circular explanation: a sentence is a complete statement; a complete statement is one that is self-supporting; it is self-supporting if it is complete; ergo: a complete statement is a statement which is complete.

Thus we are forced to abandon the "complete thought" definition since it permits us to identify sentences only by exercising our "sentence sense." But once a student has "sentence sense" he no longer needs to be taught to identify sentences, and a student who lacks this ability is unlikely to acquire it by being told that it is a "(relatively) complete thought."

The sections on German phrase and clause structure will be based on the admittedly optimistic assumption that the student of German will have a fair degree of "sentence sense" in his native English. Naturally, we thus expose ourselves to the charge of evading the issue, but since the sole purpose of this study is to find ways of helping the student to learn German better, we feel no qualms about being non-definitive on points of English grammar. (English sentence types have long been of serious concern to the linguist. Chapter 2 of Charles C. Fries' Structure of English [New York, 1952] is devoted to a discussion of the problem and its background. At present it seems that the solution will eventually be found by using the criteria of intonation patterns or in applying the methodology of transformational analysis [Noam Chomsky et al.]. The problem has turned out to be much more complicated than was at first supposed, and as of the present there is, to our knowledge, no solution which seems completely acceptable to us. Thus we feel justified in taking the stand that we do.)

Our problem here will be a discussion and classification of German sentence types. We have shown above that a definition or classification by meaning will not yield useful results. What we need are formal signs which help us in determining what "completeness" is. Perhaps we should repeat here that language is for us primarily the spoken language—which means in the present context that we are searching for signs of completeness which the student can hear. Once we have succeeded in teaching the student to recognize a sentence when he hears it spoken, and, when speaking himself, to produce an utterance which native speakers of German will accept as a sentence, we do not envisage any difficulty in applying this knowledge to the written language.

Our first classification of German sentence types will be into normal and abnormal. Since this primary division is based on pitch (or intonation) patterns it may be cessary for the reader to refer to the section on phonology which deals with intonation. J. G. Moulton, The Sounds of English and German, pp. 129-38.)

We shall call those German sentences which end with the pitch patterns . 3-1↓, . . . 2-1↓ or . . . 3-3↑, . . . 2-3↑ NORMAL SENTENCES. All sentences which ld in some other pitch pattern we shall call ABNORMAL SENTENCES.

Our reasons for doing this are that . . . 3(2)-1↓ and . . . 3(2)-3↑ seem to be erman morphemes meaning in part something like "completed utterance." Other final tch patterns do not have this meaning. Sentences with other pitch patterns include all terrupted utterances. Thus they can have any structure whatever that occurs in Ger- an. Note that we do not exclude "verbless sentences" or any other construction in Ger- an which some grammarians might consider "abnormal." Our formal criteria based on is limited number of terminal pitch patterns merely allow us to dispense with utter- nces that were interrupted by some external means or any kind of speech deficiency.

Hence, NORMAL SENTENCE TYPES can consist of any free form, i.e., ly form which is not part of a larger construction, containing the terminal morphemes . . 3(2)-1↓ or . . . 3(2)3↑. These we shall now classify further on the following basis:

) Those utterances which contain a finite verb form (in an independent clause) are MAJOR SENTENCES.

) All other utterances are MINOR SENTENCES.

1.1 | MINOR SENTENCE TYPES

We shall first deal with the minor sentences. They can be subdivided as fol- ows:

. PLAIN MINOR SENTENCES containing the morphemes . . . 3-1↓ or . . . 2-1↓.

A. Without a verb form. Examples:

Ja	Nein	Im Büro	Eine Mark zwanzig
Ruhe	Blödsinn	Guten Morgen	Ellbogen vom Tisch

This type of verbless sentence is very common in the spoken varieties of both German and English, and it is by no means as rare in the written language as is often claimed. Since English exhibits the same types of verbless sentences as German, there is no need to discuss them further.

B. With a verb form.

1. Non-finite verb form.

a. Infinitive. Examples:

Nicht hupen	Rechts halten	Rühren
Maul halten	Schneller gehen	

This type of minor sentence does not seem to exist in English, although there are no formal reasons why 'keep right,' 'be good,' 'go slow' could not contain infinitives. But the

consensus of opinion among scholars of English marks the verb forms in these sentence
as imperatives.

    b. Participial. Examples:

     Morgen geschlossen   Parken verboten
     Gut gemacht   Fertig gegessen

Here again, the German sentences are parallel to such English constructions as 'closed
today,' 'well done.' Since there is little likelihood of error on the part of the student, we
need not discuss this type of sentence any further.

    2. Finite Verb Form (in a dependent clause). Examples:

     Wenn er nur endlich käme
     Was Du nicht sagst
     Wie der immer angibt

There is a one-to-one correspondence between English and German with sentences of this
type, and no further discussion is deemed necessary. Differences in word order will be
discussed in the section on Clause Structure.

II. INTERROGATIVE MINOR SENTENCES contain the morphemes . . . 3-3↑ or . . . 2-3.
Each of the above sentence types is included here if they contain these pitch patterns. The
meaning is then something like "Is that what you said (meant, wanted)?"

   Our classification thus far has dealt with the abnormal and minor sentence
forms. Statistically they are quite uncommon in formal speech, though considerably more
frequent in informal speech. Even in the written varieties of both English and German
they appear much more often than is generally assumed. From any classificational point
of view, however, they are relatively unimportant. Moreover, we have seen that in all instances the German types of minor sentences are matched with almost exact equivalents
in the student's native language, and thus we feel that they do not warrant further discussion in this study. Much more important both from the classificational and pedagogical
viewpoints are the MAJOR SENTENCE TYPES.

   Here we use five criteria for classification, each of them set up as a binary
opposition:

1) Two pitch types: . . . 3(2)-1↓ or . . . 3(2)-3↑.
2) Two structural types: actor-action (AA), with a subject and a predicate; and action
  (A), with only a predicate.
3) Two verb forms: imperative and non-imperative. The non-imperative forms are subdivided into present subjunctive and non-present-subjunctive forms.
4) Two verb positions: First or second element in the sentence.
5) Two selection types: beginning with or without a question expression (including question words: wer, was, wie, wann, wo, warum, womit, welch-, etc.).

   Before we proceed any further with this outline of German sentence types we
should pause here to clarify once more the exact nature of this classification and the limits of its applicability (usefulness) to avoid any misunderstandings on the part of the user

This classification is based on the assumption that the following two German sentences have the same fundamental structure.

1) Er trinkt.
2) Der arme alte Mann, der gestern in völlig betrunkenem Zustande von der Polizei auf-
   gegriffen wurde und seit mehr als zehn Jahren den Behörden als unheilbar Trunksüch-
   tiger bekannt ist, trinkt bedeutend mehr als ihm bekommt, wiewohl er weiss, dass
   dieser Umstand ihn früher als unbedingt notwendig ins Grab bringen wird, wobei all
   die Schulden unbezahlt bleiben werden, die als der tiefere Grund für seine Trunksucht
   angesehen werden müssen.

That is to say: both sentences consist of subject and predicate. By using the present classification they would be grouped together as identical. The (obvious) differences between them lie not in the sentence as such, but in the structure of the constituent elements of the sentence, viz. the subject and the predicate. We shall deal with the internal structure of subject and predicate in the section on Phrase Structure.

1.2 MAJOR SENTENCE TYPES

I. With the terminal intonation morphemes . . . 2-1↓ or . . . 3-1↓.

    A. Imperative verb form.

Action only:	Komm	Komm mit	Bleibt hier
Actor-Action:	Komm du doch mit		
	Bleibt ihr doch hier		

This second type does not exist in English and the beginning student is likely to encounter difficulties here. This difficulty is best met by specially designed drills. Particular attention should be given to the fact that these Actor-Action imperative sentences will always have the sentence stress on the word which denotes the Actor (subject). Statistically, however, the actorless type of imperative sentence is much more common.

    The verb form does not have to be in first position in the sentence, though it usually is. A clause may precede:

        Wenn du Lust hast, komm mit.
        Sobald du fertig bist, ruf an.

Aside from co-ordinating conjunctions (und, aber, etc.), a small number of adverbs may precede the verb form:

        Jetzt komm schon endlich.
        Nun überlegt euch's nicht lange.

    B. Non-imperative verb form.

        1. Verb in first position.

    a.   Present subjunctive. Examples:

| Actor-Action: | Seien Sie froh |
| | Möge es Ihnen gelingen |

    b.   Non-present-subjunctive verb form. Examples:

Action only:	Friert dich	Ist dir kalt
	Wird hier viel gebaut	
Actor-Action:	Hast du Zeit	Kann er mitfahren
	Sind Sie froh	

Here we should note that there is a growing tendency among German speakers to pronounce these sentences (Type B.1.b) with the terminal pitch pattern . . . (2)3-3↑. This rising terminal contour has traditionally been prevalent in the South German standard, and during the last two decades it has become more and more frequent in the North as well. This is particularly true if the sentence can be answered by yes or no. Thus we encounter a possible contrast in such sentences as:

| Isst du zuhause | with . . . (2)3-3↑ |
| Isst du zuhause oder im Restaurant | with . . . (2)3-1↓ OR . . . (2)3-3 |

In the second example the . . . (2)3-3↑ intonation is felt to be more friendly and polite than the . . . (2)3-1↓ intonation.

    Although many verbs demand a different structure in equivalent sentences in English, most students do not usually have trouble with this German sentence type, since verbs such as <u>have</u>, <u>be</u>, and the modal auxiliaries show identical syntactic behavior in English.

    2.   Verb in second position.

        a.   Question expression first. Examples:

Action only:	Wie ist dir jetzt zumute
	Warum ist dir so kalt
	Wann wird hier endlich sauber gemacht
Actor-Action:	Wer spricht
	Wie heisst er
	Mit welchem Zug kommt er an

There is a very close resemblance between English and German with sentences of this type, and the difficulties for the learner are few, except for sentences which contain a predicate only. Special drills must be designed to meet this difficulty.

        b.   Other expression first. Examples:

Action only:	Ihn friert
	Mir ist kalt
	Jetzt wird aufgeräumt
	Wenn ich Martinis trinke, wird mir immer
	schlecht

Actor-Action: Jetzt kommt sie

Wenn sie Zeit hat, wird sie kommen

t is with this sentence type that the American student has his greatest difficulty, particu-
arly if the first element of the sentence is not the subject. This sentence type is all the
more important since it is the most common, and we will therefore devote a considerable
amount of discussion to it in the section on Clause Structure.

I. With the terminal intonation morphemes . . . 2-3↑ or . . . 3-3↑. Each of the above types
may also occur with this pitch pattern. All but Type B.1.b then have the special meaning
'Is that what you said (meant, wanted)?'' Type B.1.b may or may not have this meaning,
as we explained in the note above.

1.3 | TERMINOLOGY

Since we shall have occasion in the following sections on Phrase and Clause
structure to refer back to our classification of German sentence types, it seems convenient at this point to introduce the terms which we intend to use for the various types of
MAJOR SENTENCES which we found in German.

I. With . . . (2)3-1↓. Plain Sentences

     A. Imperative

     B. 1. a. Command

              b. Order Question

         2. a. Word Question

              b. Statement

II. With . . . (2) 3-3↑. Interrogative Sentences (''Rückfragen'').

GERMAN CLAUSES | 2

In the preceding chapter we have defined and discussed the major German sentence types. We shall now take a closer look at the major clause types which occur in German.

2.1 | DEFINITION

A clause is perhaps most simply defined as a "potential sentence." For example, the word komm "come" and the phrase er geht weg "he's going away" are both clauses. Both can also occur as complete sentences: Komm! "Come!"; Er geht weg "He's going away." On the other hand, each of them can also occur as part of a compound sentence: Komm und setz' dich! "Come and sit down"; Er geht weg, aber ich bleibe "He's going away, but I'm staying." In this case they are both still clauses; but they are no longer sentences, because they are part of still larger constructions.

2.2 | MAJOR CLAUSE TYPES

German has a great many minor clause structures, most of which can occur as complete utterances, i.e. sentences. We have dealt with these in the section on German sentence types. On the other hand, German has only two major clause types: the subject-predicate clause (Actor-Action) and the plain predicate clause (Action only). Thus, both of the major clause types contain a predicate. Since the most essential element, the center of the predicate, is always a finite verb form, we shall first have to define and list those verb forms which can occur as the center of a predicate.

2.3 | USUAL FINITE VERB FORM

We define usual finite verb form (hereafter: FV) to mean one of five forms:
1) present, e.g. bin
2) past, e.g. war
3) general subjunctive, e.g. wäre
4) special subjunctive, e.g. sei
5) imperative, e.g. sei

erhaps we should add a note here about our terminology. Most German grammar books use
e traditional terms "past subjunctive" for the general subjunctive, and "present subjunc-
ve" for the special subjunctive. These are, of course, perfectly good terms, and the pop-
arity of their use is supported both by the similarity of forms (war: wäre) and by histor-
al reasons. Nevertheless, we have decided to abandon the traditional terms in favor of
ose suggested, because we have found that our students tend to be misled by these labels.
e have encountered a great deal of trouble persuading them that the "past subjunctive"
not used as the past tense of the "present subjunctive." It is this difficulty which we try
avoid by choosing our terms.

2.4 | ARRANGEMENTS WITHIN THE CLAUSE

In analyzing German clauses we find that there is considerable freedom of ar-
ngement. The German equivalent of "Mr. Meyer goes to town every morning" can occur
ith its constituents arranged in five (and only five) different ways.

1. Herr Meyer fährt jeden Morgen in die Stadt
2

2. jeden Morgen fährt Herr Meyer in die Stadt
2

3. in die Stadt fährt Herr Meyer jeden Morgen
2

4. fährt Herr Meyer jeden Morgen in die Stadt
1

5. Herr Meyer jeden Morgen in die Stadt fährt
L

e note that the usual finite verb form occurs in second position in numbers 1, 2, and 3 —
d thus we conclude that as clause types, numbers 1, 2, and 3 are identical. Number 4 is
different type, because it is a question rather than a statement. Its essential feature is
e fact that the usual finite verb form is in first position. Number 5 is again different, be-
ause it is a dependent clause structure: "(wenn, weil, ob, etc.) Herr Meyer jeden Morgen
die Stadt fährt."

If we use the position of the usual finite verb form as our sole criterion, it is
vident that we arrive at three basic clause types. We have grouped together numbers 1,
, and 3, because their essential feature is that the FV is in second position. We can label
is clause type FV-2, and name it "Statement." The clause type illustrated by number 4
e shall label FV-1, and name it "Order question." Similarly, we shall label the type il-
ustrated by number 5 FV-L and name it "Dependent clause."

2.41 WHAT IS A CLAUSE ELEMENT?

FV-2 is without a doubt the most common of German clause types. Since it is
lso one of the most difficult for native speakers of English it deserves a good deal of at-
ntion. Before we proceed to a discussion of the various subdivisions of this type, let us
ause here and direct our attention to the essential points of difference between English

and German clause structure. This difference shows up most clearly if we attempt to gi[v]
verbatim translations of examples 1-3.

1. Mr. Meyer goes to town every morning.[1]
2. Every morning Mr. Meyer goes to town.
3. To town Mr. Meyer goes every morning.

If we assume that number 3 is possible as a clause in English (although it is[i]
very close to our limits of tolerance), then the point which we wish to make becomes
clear: in clauses of this type, English structure demands that the subject precede the finite verb form, i.e. the position of the finite verb element is flexible in contrast to German. It follows then that the student will encounter little difficulty when confronted with
clause structured like number 1—but he will be confused by any German clause in which
the first element is not the subject. In other words, position 2, the position of the usual
finite verb form, functions as the pivot of any "statement-clause" in German. This fact [i]
easily explained to any student—but the explanation will not do much good until the stude[nt]
has acquired the habit of uttering the finite verb form immediately after the first eleme[nt]
This habit can be learned only by extensive drills—involving clauses with many element[s]
which the student is required to rearrange. Let us take a closer look at an example whic[h]
is deliberately complicated to show many different arrangements:

1. sie $\underset{\text{FV-2}}{\underline{\text{soll}}}$ ihm gestern nicht gern geholfen haben

2. ihm $\underset{\text{FV-2}}{\underline{\text{soll}}}$ sie gestern nicht gern geholfen haben

3. gestern $\underset{\text{FV-2}}{\underline{\text{soll}}}$ sie ihm nicht gern geholfen haben

4. gern $\underset{\text{FV-2}}{\underline{\text{soll}}}$ sie ihm gestern nicht geholfen haben

5. geholfen haben $\underset{\text{FV-2}}{\underline{\text{soll}}}$ sie ihm gestern nicht gern

* 6. nicht gern $\underset{\text{FV-2}}{\underline{\text{soll}}}$ sie ihm gestern geholfen haben

* 7. geholfen $\underset{\text{FV-2}}{\underline{\text{soll}}}$ sie ihm gestern nicht gern haben

** 8. nicht $\underset{\text{FV-2}}{\underline{\text{soll}}}$ sie ihm gestern gern geholfen haben

** 9. haben $\underset{\text{FV-2}}{\underline{\text{soll}}}$ sie ihm gestern nicht gern geholfen

By rearranging this clause we find that there are limitations in regard to the number of
possibilities. Any speaker of German will accept the first five variations as perfectly no[r]
mal renderings of the clause "it looked like she didn't want to help him yesterday." Ther[e]
will be some reluctance to consider numbers 6 and 7 as normal, but the native speaker
will readily admit that they are at least "grammatical." Numbers 8 and 9, on the other
hand, turn out to be non-acceptable even by the most tolerant of native speakers. Since w[e]

---

1. The different sequence of "to town every morning" vs. "jeden Morgen in
die Stadt" we shall discuss in the chapter dealing with the order of clause elements.

fine as a clause element any word or group of words which can precede the usual finite rb form in a statement (FV-2) clause, it follows that <u>nicht</u> and <u>haben</u> are not elements the clause which we have examined. The reason for this is, of course, that both <u>nicht</u> d <u>haben</u> are parts of phrases: <u>nicht gern</u> and <u>geholfen haben</u> respectively. This fact by elf, however, is not reason enough: numbers 4 and 7 prove that the other constituents these two phrases can take position one, and thus function as elements. Further study ows that <u>nicht</u> can never function as an element, whereas <u>haben</u> (or any other infinitive) n, unless it is an immediate constituent of a participal phrase. We can now summarize r findings on clause elements:

A clause element may consist of a word. Examples:

> <u>dort</u> geht sie
> <u>ich</u> bin es
> <u>nie</u> kommt er rechtzeitig zur Probe
> <u>wo</u> ist der Bahnhof

A clause element may consist of a phrase. Examples:

> <u>frische Butter</u> ist teuer
> <u>die zwei weissen Häuser</u> können Sie doch sehen
> <u>eines Tages</u> ist es dann zu spät
> <u>das Buch meines Lehrers</u> hat mir am besten gefallen

A clause element may be expanded by an adverb which follows. Examples:

> <u>am Morgen erst</u> kam er an
> <u>am Morgen freilich</u> erfuhr er es
> <u>am Morgen schliesslich</u> wussten sie es
> <u>am Morgen noch</u> muss es erledigt werden
> <u>am Morgen zwar</u> ist es zu spät

A clause element may consist of an entire clause. Examples:

a)   dependent clauses

> <u>als er endlich ankam</u> war es zu spät
> <u>ob er mitkommen darf</u> wollte ich fragen
> <u>wer nicht mitmacht</u> ist ein Spielverderber
> <u>der hier wohnt</u> arbeitet beim Stadtrat

b)   independent clauses

> <u>hört doch endlich damit auf</u> rief die Mutter
> <u>wo waren Sie gestern abend</u> wollte der Inspektor wissen
> <u>ich bin es nicht gewesen</u> sagte er immer wieder

Certain adverbs may not usually function as clause elements. Examples:

1.   nicht
2.   sehr
3.   ausschliesslich

But: <u>fast</u> könnte man sagen, dass . . . etc.

2.42 FV-2 CLAUSES

We have seen that this clause type is the commonest of all German clauses and that the main difficulty with it—as far as the native speaker of English is concerne is the fact that the position of the usual finite verb form is fixed, whereas first positio be occupied by any clause element. As a name for this type we have suggested "statem clause."

Statements may be of the actor-action type, i.e. contain both a subject and predicate or, less commonly, they may be of the action type, i.e. contain only a predica Examples for the actor-action type have been given in the preceding paragraphs. Exam ples containing only a predicate follow:

1. hier <u>wird</u> sonntags getanzt
   FV-2

2. mich <u>friert</u> immer beim Skifahren
   FV-2

3. in den Nachkriegsjahren <u>wurde</u> in München viel gebaut
   FV-2

4. meinem Mann <u>ist</u> auch kalt
   FV-2

5. nach dem Unfallkommando <u>ist</u> schon geschickt worden[2]
   FV-2

It is evident to any teacher of German that these actorless clauses represent a source much confusion to the learner since no equivalent clause type exists in his native langu Special drills have to be designed to meet this difficulty. With the clauses containing fo of <u>werden</u> plus a participle it has proved helpful to base the drills on a variation in whi <u>es</u> occupies position one. For example:

1) es wurde in den Nachkriegsjahren in München viel gebaut
2) in München wurde in den Nachkriegsjahren viel gebaut, etc.

It seems that the student thus profits by the similarity to other constructio involving <u>es</u>, e.g. es gibt viele Häuser in München.

So far all the FV-2 clauses which we have examined have been declarative, and thus our suggested name for this clause type, "statement," has been appropriate. W find, however, that there are a great many occurrences of the FV-2 clause in which the first element is a question word or a phrase built around a question word. Examples:

Actor-Action   wie <u>heisst</u> er
        QW   2

         wann <u>kommt</u> der Zug an
        QW   2

         mit welchem Zug <u>kommt</u> er an
           QW   2

---

2. The clauses involving <u>werden</u> + participle are, of course, passives. For further discussion of passives, see Sec. 3 on Phrase Structure.

Action $\underset{QW}{\text{wieso}}\ \underset{2}{\text{ist}}$ Ihnen komisch zumute

$\underset{QW}{\text{warum}}\ \underset{2}{\text{wird}}$ ihr beim Weintrinken immer schlecht

$\text{aus}\ \underset{QW}{\underline{\text{welchen Gründen}}}\ \underset{2}{\text{war}}$ ihm kalt

e suggest the name "Word Question" for this type of FV-2 clauses since its essential ature is the presence of a question word or phrase. This latter usually is the first ele- ent, though this is not essential, as witness the example:

er $\underset{2}{\text{sagte}}\ \underset{QW}{\text{was}}$?

2.5 OCCURRENCE OF SUBJUNCTIVES

Our examples so far have had as their usual finite verb form only forms of ie present or past. However, as pointed out in §2.3, forms of the general or special sub- inctive may also function as the FV, though they are, of course, much less common than ither the present or the past. In a context where indirect quote is possible, the FV may e in either the general or the special subjunctive. We find the same clause types which e have discussed. Examples: (Wir sprachen über Tante Elses Besuch)

1)   sie $\underset{2}{\text{würde}}$ (werde) morgen früh ankommen (FV-2, Statement, actor-action)

2)   nach der Bahnfahrt $\underset{2}{\text{wäre}}$ (sei) ihr gewöhnlich nicht sehr wohl (FV-2, state-
                                             ment, action)

3)   an $\underset{QW}{\underline{\text{welchem Bahnhof}}}\ \underset{2}{\text{käme}}$ (komme) sie denn an (FV-2, word question,
                                             actor-action)

4) $\underset{QW}{\text{weshalb}}\ \underset{2}{\text{würde}}$ (werde) ihr denn immer schlecht beim Bahnfahren (FV-2,
                                             word question, action)

2.51 SPECIAL SUBJUNCTIVE: SS—1-2 CLAUSES

Sometimes the usual finite verb occurs in the form of the special subjunctive SS) in contexts where an indirect quote is not indicated. The special subjunctive form is sually the second element in such clauses, but it is not at all uncommon to find it in first osition without change of meaning. Examples:

Actor-Action   man $\underset{SS}{\text{nehme}}$ zweihundert Gramm Butter

danach $\underset{SS}{\text{nehme}}$ man 200 Gramm Butter

Gott $\underset{SS}{\text{gebe}}$, dass . . .

$\underset{SS}{\text{möge}}$ ihm gelingen (was er sich vorgenommen hat)

ihm $\underset{SS}{\text{möge}}$ gelingen (was anderen misslang)

This type is most commonly used as the equivalent of the imperative (see below). The s[ ]cial subjunctive is then usually (though not always) the first element, and the pronoun su[ ]ject follows it immediately:

Actor-Action
$$\underset{\text{SS}}{\text{seien}} \text{ Sie froh}$$
$$\underset{\text{SS}}{\text{seien}} \text{ wir froh}$$
$$\text{jetzt } \underset{\text{SS}}{\text{seien}} \text{ Sie ruhig}$$
$$\text{jetzt } \underset{\text{SS}}{\text{seien}} \text{ wir ruhig}$$

The essential feature of this clause type is the use of a special subjunctive in contexts where an indirect quote is not indicated. Since the position of the usual finite verb form may be either first or second, we suggest the label SS−1-2 for this clause type. "Command" suggests itself as a convenient name, but it should be remembered that we wish t[ ]keep this clause type separate from "imperative clauses." Note furthermore that this ty[ ]of clause is often not clearly marked since only the verb sein has a special subjunctive form which is clearly distinguished from the present indicative forms. Taken out of con[ ]text, and without the benefit of intonation markers (see section on Favorite Sentence Typ[ ]the forms of other verbs are ambiguous: The utterance "bleiben Sie hier" can be either command (SS-1) or an order question (FV-1, see below).

We have seen that the structure of subjunctive clauses does not essentially differ from that of indicative clauses. Thus, from a pedagogical point of view they are mainly bothersome not as clauses, but because the learner either does not recognize the[ ]subjunctive forms when he meets them in his reading or—in speaking—fails to use such forms when the context demands them. The first problem we may meet by extensive dri[ ]on the verb forms by either substitution or completion exercises. The second difficulty c[ ]best be overcome by contrastive drills, setting off cases of direct quote from those of in[ ]direct quote. As teachers we may take comfort in the tendency of present-day speakers [ ]German to exhibit a growing inclination to avoid the use of the special subjunctive—re[ ]serving it more and more for very formal varieties of the written language.

2.6 IMPERATIVE CLAUSES

In many ways this clause type is similar to the one discussed in the precedin[ ]section. Its essential feature is that the usual finite verb form is an imperative. Most commonly this verb form is the first element of the clause, but this need not be so: an ad[ ]verb or another clause may precede. With this clause type the "action only" variety is th[ ]more frequent, and so we list it first.

Action
$$\underset{\text{IMP}}{\text{komm}}$$
$$\underset{\text{IMP}}{\text{bleibt}} \text{ hier}$$
$$\text{jetzt } \underset{\text{IMP}}{\text{komm}} \text{ schon endlich}$$
$$\text{wenn du Lust hast } \underset{\text{IMP}}{\text{komm}} \text{ mit}$$

Actor-Action   hilf du ihm doch
                  ‾IMP‾

                  bleibt ihr doch hier
                  ‾IMP‾

the less common actor-action type, ambiguity would be possible because the plural im-
erative (e.g. bleibt) is identical in form with the 2d person plural present indicative (al-
o bleibt). This is usually avoided by the insertion of the lexical item doch to mark the
ommand.

A further distinguishing feature of the actor-action type is the fact that the
ersonal pronoun which always immediately follows the verb form bears the clause stress,
e. the point of greatest loudness falls invariably on this pronoun.

The common action-only type presents no difficulty to the learner since his
ative English makes use of an identical pattern. The actor-action type will have to be
rilled specially.

2.7 | ORDER QUESTIONS: FV-1 CLAUSES

The last one of the independent clause types which we need to discuss is the
rder question, a clause type the essential feature of which is that the usual finite verb
orm occurs in first position. Although this is a very common major clause type in Ger-
an our discussion can be brief since the sole difference between this type and the state-
ent is the position of the verb; all other features apply equally to both types. In other
ords, the only transformation the student has to perform is a simple regrouping of the
lause elements. Examples:

Actor-Action   geht sie dort
                  ‾V-1‾

                  ist frische Butter teuer
                  ‾V-1‾

                  kam er erst am Morgen an
                  ‾V-1‾

Action only   wird sonntags hier getanzt
                  ‾V-1‾

                  ist nach dem Unfallkommando schon geschickt worden
                  ‾V-1‾

                  ist dir kalt
                  ‾V-1‾

t would seem that this clause type with the FV in first position does not present any dif-
iculties to learners whose native language is English since they are quite familiar with
his clause arrangement in their own language. Examples:

sind Sie zu Hause   are you home
‾FV-1‾   ‾FV-1‾

soll ich gehen   shall I go
‾FV-1‾   ‾FV-1‾

$$\underset{\text{FV-1}}{\underline{\text{muss}}} \text{ er es wissen} \qquad \underset{\text{FV-1}}{\underline{\text{must}}} \text{ he know (it)}$$

All of these verbs are, of course, auxiliaries—thus, all we should have to do is to point out to the student that <u>all</u> interrogative clauses in German (conveniently) follow this sam pattern. Unfortunately, as any teacher knows, the matter is not as simple as this. Our s dents have deep-seated grammatical habits of clearly (if not always consciously) keepin auxiliaries separate from all other verbs, and it is the vastly different behavior of all these other verbs which forms the basis for the interference which the student has to overcome. Compare these clauses:

$$\text{er } \underset{\text{FV-2}}{\underline{\text{arbeitet}}} \text{ gewöhnlich in der Bibliothek}$$

he usually works in the library

$$\underset{\text{FV-1}}{\underline{\text{arbeitet}}} \text{ er gewöhnlich in der Bibliothek}$$

$$\underset{\text{AUX}}{\underline{\text{does}}} \text{ he usually } \underset{\text{V}}{\underline{\text{work}}} \text{ in the library}$$

In a very real sense, then, the FV-1 arrangement is an entirely new construction for ou students since his customary interrogative clause has the construction:

<u>AUXILIARY</u> + SUBJECT + <u>INFINITIVE</u>

English grammar demands an auxiliary before the subject in both affirmative and nega- tive questions unless the subject is one of the interrogative subjects Who? What? Which (+noun)? This latter type we have labeled Word Question, and in the discussion (§2.42) w found that in German grammar it can most easily be dealt with as a sub-class of the FV clause type.

Our examples above have shown that the copula and all auxiliaries except <u>DC</u> do not interfere with learning the German clause type which we labeled Order Question. Thus we can now pinpoint the feature of English grammar which causes our troubles witl this German clause type: it is the occurrence of the so-called "empty" auxiliary <u>DO</u>, anc our task as teachers is to replace that pattern by the corresponding German pattern:

DO + SUBJECT + INFINITIVE (of full verb) ⟶
FV (of full verb) + SUBJECT, etc.

We feel that the best way to do this is by a series of graded drills in which the student is required to make questions out of statements. Since we want to take advantage of the pos itive transfer afforded by clauses involving the copula and the auxiliaries (other than <u>DO</u> we will start with such clauses. Only when the student has gained fluency with these will we introduce clauses involving "full verbs" with the <u>DO</u> construction. For example:

he can come	er kann kommen
$\underset{\text{FV-1}}{\underline{\text{can}}}$ he come	$\underset{\text{FV-1}}{\underline{\text{kann}}}$ er kommen, <u>etc.</u>
he works	er arbeitet
$\underset{\text{DO}}{\underline{\text{does}}}$ he $\underset{\text{INF}}{\underline{\text{work}}}$	$\underset{\text{FV-1}}{\underline{\text{arbeitet}}}$ er, <u>etc.</u>

2.8 | DEPENDENT CLAUSES: FV-L

In the preceding paragraphs we have analyzed and discussed all the major independent clause types in German, and how—in our opinion—their characteristics can
most easily be made familiar to our students. The remainder of this section will be devoted to a discussion of dependent clauses.

Their common characteristic and essential feature is, as we all know, that
the usual finite verb form usually occupies the last position in the clause.

There are four major types of dependent clauses, and all of them can best be
described and taught if we consider them as transforms, i.e. results of transformations,
of our major types of independent clauses. So far our procedure has been to always begin
with the most frequent type of clause, but this time we start our discussion with one of
the less common types: the dependent clause introduced by a question word (QW + FV-L).
We do this, as every teacher of German immediately realizes, because this type shows
an almost identical word order in English. Compare:

> Can you tell me: "Where is the station?"
> Can you tell me where the station is?

2.81 CLAUSE INTRODUCER: QUESTION WORD

The essential features of this clause type are that the first position is filled
by a question word, and that the usual finite verb form occupies the last position. As we
have mentioned, this clause type is the transform of the "word question" (QW + FV-2).
Examples:

Actor-Action
QW - FV-2 $\underset{\text{QW}}{\underline{\text{wessen}}}$ Hut $\underset{\text{FV-2}}{\underline{\text{ist}}}$ das

Transform:
QW + FV-L $\underset{\text{QW}}{\underline{\text{wessen}}}$ Hut das $\underset{\text{FV-L}}{\underline{\text{ist}}}$

QW + FV-L $\underset{\text{QW}}{\underline{\text{mit welchem Zug}}}$ er ankommt

Action only $\underset{\text{QW}}{\underline{\text{warum}}}$ ihr beim Weintrinken immer schlecht $\underset{\text{FV-L}}{\underline{\text{wird}}}$

                   $\underset{\text{QW}}{\underline{\text{aus welchen Gründen}}}$ gestern nicht gearbeitet $\underset{\text{FV-L}}{\underline{\text{wurde}}}$

If we take a closer look at the English pattern of this type we find, of course,
that the similarity which we cited in §2.8 does not go very far, and consequently the student will encounter strong interference which we shall have to overcome. Compare these
examples:

| | John arbeitet gewöhnlich in der Bibliothek |
| (Können Sie mir sagen $\underset{\text{QW-1}}{\underline{\text{warum}}}$) | John gewöhnlich in der Bibliothek $\underset{\text{FV-L}}{\underline{\text{arbeitet}}}$ |

John usually works in the library

Can you tell me why   John usually works in the library

We have seen that most questions in English use the DO + SUBJECT + INFINITIVE construction (see §2.7). Even if we leave this problem aside for the moment we find that in indirect questions introduced by a question word, English structure demands a formula quite different from the German pattern. We may phrase it, somewhat vaguely, like this:

QW + (whatever can precede the FV in a statement) + FV

That is to say: within the framework of English an indirect question involving a QW is most easily formed when it is based on the underlying <u>statement</u>, and <u>not</u> on the underlying <u>direct question</u>, e.g.:

Statement   (1) John works at home

Indirect Question: (2) . . . why John works at home

Direct question: (3) why does John work at home

Whereas in English (3) differs radically from (1) and (2), German grammar allows us to group together (1) and (3) since both share the feature of FV-2. On the other hand, (2) in German involves the formula QW-1 + FV-L which is obligatory and does not allow of any variation, e.g.

Statement: (1) John $\underset{\text{FV-2}}{\underline{\text{arbeitet}}}$ zuhause

Indirect Question: (2) . . . $\underset{\text{QW-1}}{\underline{\text{warum}}}$ John zuhause $\underset{\text{FV-L}}{\underline{\text{arbeitet}}}$

Direct question: (3) $\underset{\text{QW-1}}{\underline{\text{warum}}}$ arbeitet John $\underset{\text{FV-2}}{\underline{\text{zuhause}}}$

Since our goal is to teach the student the required word order in German indirect questions, we shall have to organize our drills in such a way as to avoid the additional confusion caused by the structure of English (2): (QW) + DO + SUBJECT + INFINITIVE. Our pattern drills will therefore have as their starting point English statements and <u>not</u> English direct questions. (On the other end, if we choose to drill entirely in German, it would seem more reasonable to use direct questions as our starting point.) Examples:

1a. John works at home   John $\underset{\text{FV-2}}{\underline{\text{arbeitet}}}$ zuhause

1b. . . . why John works at home   . . . warum John zuhause $\underset{\text{FV-L}}{\underline{\text{arbeitet}}}$

2a. Mary plays basketball   Mary $\underset{\text{FV-2}}{\underline{\text{spielt}}}$ Korbball

2b. . . . when Mary plays basketball . . . wann Mary Korbball $\underset{\text{FV-L}}{\underline{\text{spielt}}}$, etc.

2.82 CLAUSE INTRODUCER: SUBORDINATING CONJUNCTION (SUB)

The dependent clause introduced by a SUB is easily the most frequent, and thus it accounts for a good many mistakes which our students make in regard to word order. The reason for this is, of course, that English word order does not undergo any changes if a clause is subordinated to another clause. In fact, many of our students have a good deal of trouble distinguishing subordinate clauses from main clauses. This clause type (as well as the relative clause, see below) can most easily be described as the transform of the statement clause. Examples:

Actor-Action

FV-2   er $\underline{\text{fährt}}$ in die Stadt
                 $\overline{\text{FV-2}}$

Transform:

SUB + FV-L   (weil) er in die Stadt $\underline{\text{fährt}}$
            $\overline{\text{SUB}}$ $\overline{\text{FV-L}}$

                 (obwohl) sie morgen $\underline{\text{kommt}}$
            $\overline{\text{SUB}}$ $\overline{\text{FV-L}}$

                 (wenn) wir erst genug Geld $\underline{\text{haben}}$
            $\overline{\text{SUB}}$ $\overline{\text{FV-L}}$

Action only   (damit) hier getanzt werden $\underline{\text{kann}}$
            $\overline{\text{SUB}}$ $\overline{\text{FV-L}}$

                 (weil) meinem Mann auch zu kalt $\underline{\text{ist}}$
            $\overline{\text{SUB}}$ $\overline{\text{FV-L}}$

2.821 CLAUSE INTRODUCER: RELATIVE PRONOUN (REL)

This dependent clause type introduced by a relative pronoun is again a transform of the statement clause—and the difficulties we have mentioned in the preceding paragraph apply here as well.

Actor-Action

FV-2   der $\underline{\text{fährt}}$ in die Stadt
                 $\overline{\text{FV-2}}$

Transform:

REL + FV-L $\underline{\text{der}}$ in die Stadt $\underline{\text{fährt}}$
            $\overline{\text{REL}}$ $\overline{\text{FV-L}}$

                 $\underline{\text{dessen}}$ Sohn auf der Universität $\underline{\text{studiert}}$
            $\overline{\text{REL}}$ $\overline{\text{FV-L}}$

                 $\underline{\text{denen}}$ ich die Bücher geliehen $\underline{\text{habe}}$
            $\overline{\text{REL}}$ $\overline{\text{FV-L}}$

Action only

FV-2   ihm ist immer schlecht

Transform:

REL + FV-L $\underline{\text{dem}}$ immer schlecht $\underline{\text{ist}}$
            $\overline{\text{REL}}$ $\overline{\text{FV-L}}$

                 $\underline{\text{den}}$ im Freien immer $\underline{\text{friert}}$
            $\overline{\text{REL}}$ $\overline{\text{FV-L}}$

2.822 CLAUSE INTRODUCER: OB "WHETHER"

A dependent clause introduced by $\underline{\text{OB}}$ differs from those described in the preceding paragraphs in that it is best analyzed as the transform of an order question, i.e. a clause in which the usual finite verb form is in first position (see §2.7). In all other respects this clause duplicates the structure of the other dependent clauses.

Actor-Action

FV-1 $\underline{kommt}$ er morgen
               $\overline{FV}$

Transform:

OB + FV-L $\underline{ob}$ er morgen $\underline{kommt}$
                                            $\overline{FV}$

                $\underline{ob}$ er für uns Zeit $\underline{hat}$
                                                 $\overline{FV}$

Action only $\underline{wird}$ ihm leicht übel
                $\overline{FV}$

OB + FV-L $\underline{ob}$ ihm leicht übel $\underline{wird}$
                                                 $\overline{FV}$

As in teaching the word order of the other dependent clauses, it has proved most useful here to spend a minimum of time explaining the structure. Instead we have found that drills bring the essential point much more quickly to the student. Drills for the ob-clause can most easily be designed within frames like Fragen Sie ihn doch nochmal, ob . . . "why don't you ask him again whether. . . ." Note that English allows us to substitute the (probably less elegant) if for the clause introducer whether without any change of meaning. For example: "I don't know if (whether) he's coming." This flexibility in English leads student to say things like ich weiss nicht, wenn er kommt, which is, of course, wrong. We must point out to our students that the German wenn can never substitute for ob: its meaning is restricted to "whenever," and "if = on condition that."

2.823 DEPENDENT CLAUSE WITHOUT CLAUSE INTRODUCER

We are left with a type of dependent clause which in structure is identical to the clause which we have named "order question" (§2.7). Its status as a dependent clause is marked solely by the fact that it must be followed by another clause which may be introduced by so or dann. This second clause (the main clause) begins with the usual finite verb form although it is not an order question. Thus we conclude that position 1 of the main clause is taken by the dependent clause under discussion and that so and dann (if they do occur) function as non-elements in this context.

This clause type would present a good many teaching problems were it not for the fact that English structure permits a very similar clause type:

Had I seen him, I should have told him about it.

It should be noted however, that this English clause type is semantically restricted. It may occur only in so-called conditions contrary to fact. No such restriction exists for the equivalent German clause type. This does, of course, not detract from the usefulness of the pedagogical device of beginning our presentation of this German clause type by making our students aware of the English pattern. We may even go so far as to suggest that the subordinating conjunction wenn (respectively "if") has been left out and the finite verb

...m put in its stead—though linguistically we have no way of showing that anything has ...en left out.

<table>
<tr><td>Actor-Action</td><td>fährt er jeden Morgen in die Stadt, (so, dann) . . .
FV-1   FV-2</td></tr>
</table>

Actor-Action $\underline{\text{fährt}}$ er jeden Morgen in die Stadt, (so, dann) . . . $\underline{\text{FV-2}}$
                FV-1

                           $\underline{\text{weiss}}$ sie genug, (dann) . . . $\underline{\text{FV-2}}$
                            FV-1

Action only $\underline{\text{wird}}$ genug geleistet, (dann) . . . $\underline{\text{FV-2}}$
                            FV-1

                            $\underline{\text{ist}}$ Ihnen immer kalt, (so) . . . $\underline{\text{FV-2}}$
                            FV-1

2.9 | NEGATION

Any one of the various clause types which we have discussed in the preceding ...ragraphs can, of course, be affirmative or negative. All our examples so far have been ...the affirmative type in order to postpone the problem of clause negation which we want ...discuss here. If we were to stay strictly within the limits of German clause grammar, ...en there would be no problem: A speaker of German can negate any affirmative clause ...mply by the insertion of $\underline{\text{nicht}}$, e.g.

er wird mitgehen   ⟶   er wird $\underset{\text{NEG}}{\underline{\text{nicht}}}$ mitgehen

er arbeitet zuhause   ⟶   er arbeitet $\underset{\text{NEG}}{\underline{\text{nicht}}}$ zuhause

...e difficulties which our students face when confronted with negative clauses become ap-...rent only when we contrast the German clauses with their English equivalents:

he will come along   ⟶   he will $\underset{\text{NEG}}{\underline{\text{not}}}$ (won't) come along

he works at home   ⟶   he $\underset{\text{DO}}{\underline{\text{does}}}$ $\underset{\text{NEG}}{\underline{\text{not}}}$ work at home

...nce again we find (as we did in the discussion of Order Questions, §2.7) that the peculiar ...ammatical characteristics of the English verb auxiliaries will tend to interfere with the ...udent's learning of the German pattern. The transfer will readily be made in clauses ...ich contain a modal auxiliary or the copula $\underline{\text{be}}$, since in these clauses the grammatical ...ructures of the two languages are compatible. But if, on the other hand, the English ...ause is negated by the "empty" modal $\underline{\text{DO}}$ (plus negative), the student has to learn an en-...rely new pattern which—despite its apparent simplicity—runs counter to all the gram-...atical habits which his native English has instilled in him. We shall have to meet this ...oblem by a series of graded drills, starting with English clauses involving modal aux-...aries, continuing with clauses in which a "plain" verb form occurs, and ending up with ...auses involving gerund forms. Examples:

1. he can't fly   ⟶   er kann nicht fliegen, $\underline{\text{etc}}$.
2. he doesn't work   ⟶   er arbeitet nicht, $\underline{\text{etc}}$.
3. he isn't coming   ⟶   er kommt nicht, $\underline{\text{etc}}$.

PHRASE STRUCTURE | 3

3.0 | INTRODUCTORY

We should start this section by stating that the English and German phrase structures are remarkably similar and that the areas of conflict are few. Therefore mu of our discussion can be quite brief—we shall go into detail only where our students are likely to encounter difficulties.

A PHRASE is any construction made up of two or more words. German, jus like English, has four common types of phrase structure: (1) Subordinate Structure, (2) ordinate Structure (conjunction), (3) Coordinate Structure (apposition), (4) Centerless St ture.

3.1 | SUBORDINATE STRUCTURE: CENTER ←MODIFIER

In the sentence he speaks, he is called the subject, speaks the predicate. If expand this to he speaks well, we find that the phrase speaks well performs exactly the same function as the word speaks. We therefore say that speaks and well are in constru tion with each other, and that speaks is the CENTER of the phrase, well is its MODIFIE We can symbolize this by writing speaks ← well; with an arrow pointing from the modif er to the center. If we expand this still further to he speaks very well, we find that the phrase very well performs exactly the same function as the word well. We therefore wr very → well. And the whole predicate now has the structure speaks ← (very → well). In all three of these examples we may say that speaks is the center of the predicate, either alone: speaks, or with a modifying word: speaks well, or with a modifying phrase: speak very well.

The term EXPRESSION is customarily used to include both words and phras Thus a "verbal expression" is either a verb or a phrase with a verb as a center; an "ad verbial expression" is either an adverb or a phrase with adverb as center; etc. We shal shorten these lengthy labels to simple "verbal," "adverbial," etc. In the above example, well and very well are both adverbials; and speaks, speaks well, speaks very well are a verbals.

3.10(a) ATTRIBUTIVE MODIFIERS

These are modifiers like those in the examples used above. In both English and German they may be either words (alone or expanded), certain phrases, or clauses.

(a) ATTRIBUTIVE WORDS. German has four classes, all of which are matched by comparable English equivalents.

(i) ADVERBIALS modify nearly all types of expressions, e.g. verbals steht ← f 'gets up'; nominals nur → Geld ' only money'; pronominals selbst → ich 'even I'; ad-ctivals sehr → dunkel 'very dark'; and other adverbials fast → immer 'almost always.'

The major point of conflict with English structure arises with certain kinds of verbials which modify verbals (so-called stressed adverbs, separable prefixes). Two istakes are made fairly commonly: In generating a German clause involving such a rase, the student will tend to have the adverb follow immediately after the verb it modi-ᵉs since this is what the structure of his native English usually demands in such a case. ᵉrman word order, on the other hand, usually places the adverbial at the very end of the ause in which it occurs, although there is a growing tendency in modern German to put ᵉ adverb at the end of the "thought" rather than the clause, e.g.

er $\underset{\text{FV}}{\underline{\text{kommt}}}$ mit seinem Geld trotz aller Schwierigkeiten $\underset{\text{ADV}}{\underline{\text{aus}}}$ =

er $\underset{\text{FV}}{\underline{\text{kommt}}}$ mit seinem Geld $\underset{\text{ADV}}{\underline{\text{aus}}}$ trotz aller Schwierigkeiten

'he stays within his budget in spite of all the difficulties'

In discussing such German phrases it is generally useful to mention that Eng-ᵇh word order can be varied without change of meaning. For example:

he puts his clothes on
he puts on his clothes

Another problem caused by the peculiar German word order frequently shows in reading. Since English grammar almost always has the adverb closely following the rb which it modifies, the student fails to realize that he has to keep an "open mind" in gard to the verb until he reaches the end of the clause, since the modifying adverb more ᵗen than not changes the meaning of the verb. Almost any German verb can be modified an adverbial, and thus we must always insist that the entire clause be read through be-ᵣe an attempt at translation is made; better yet, we should try to avoid translation alto-ther and instead aim at a "tacit" understanding of the German clause.

The second mistake which we mentioned above is of a less serious nature ᵑce it is only a question of spelling. The rules of German orthography demand that the rbal and modifying adverbial be written together whenever the adverb immediately pre-des the verbal. Thus we get:

er steht auf	'he gets up'
er sollte aufstehen	'he should get up'
er hat aufzustehen	'he has to get up'
er ist aufgestanden	'he got up'

ᵉ should point out that most dictionaries list these so-called "compound verbs" under ᵉ adverbial since the listing is based on the infinitive. In making this orthographic pe-.liarity more easily understandable to the student we have found it helpful to remind ᵉm of similar inconsistencies in English: e.g. another boy vs. the other boy.

(ii) ADJECTIVALS modify nominals: <u>ein</u> → <u>Mann</u> 'a man," <u>dieses</u> → <u>Hotel</u> 'this hotel,' <u>heisser</u> → <u>Kaffee</u> 'hot coffee,' <u>meine</u> → (<u>neuen</u> → <u>Schuhe</u>) 'my new shoes,' <u>die</u> → (<u>zwei</u> → <u>weissen</u> → <u>Häuser</u>) 'the two white houses'; and also other adjectivals: <u>meine</u> → <u>neuen</u> 'my new ones,' <u>die</u> → (<u>zwei</u> → <u>weissen</u>) 'the two white ones.'

As the examples show, these phrases are equally common in English. Differ ences arise mainly from the fact that German grammar demands that the adjectival "agree" with the nominal. We will discuss this question in more detail in the section on Compulsory Grammatical Categories.

There is, however, one German phrase type involving the modification of a nominal by an adjectival which causes a great deal of trouble in reading expository pros Our grammar books call this type of phrase variously "extended adjective construction," extended participial phrase," etc. Its essential feature is that the adjectival is itself mo ified. This feature is, of course, quite common in English also, e.g.:

> an extremely important area
> a relatively unknown composer
> the previously described case

But English structure is very restrictive in regard to the kind and number of modifiers used in such phrases. German, on the other hand, has practically no limitations on the kinds and number of modifiers which may precede the nominal. We reach beyond the lim its of English phrase structure if we wish to extend this type of phrase to read:

> *a to me unknown composer
> *a here unknown composer

In German the equivalents are perfectly possible:

> ein mir unbekannter Komponist
> ein hier unbekannter Komponist

If we wish to translate such phrases into English we have to resort to a different type of construction:

> a composer unknown to me
> a composer unknown in this country (here)

Even so, the second example sounds a bit clumsy, and we may have to use a full relative clause in our translation:

> a composer who is unknown in this country (here)

In many cases the full relative clause is the only way in which we can translate the Ger man phrase:

> meine kürzlich verstorbene Tante
> my aunt <u>who</u> died recently [but not]
> *my aunt died recently

In German as in English the nominal may be modified by one or more inde pendent adjectives in addition to the extended adjectival.

a relatively unknown young composer
ein verhältnissmässig unbekannter junger Komponist

omplications arise when English structure demands that the modified adjectival follow
e noun, whereas the independent adjectival must precede the noun. Compare these two
rases:

das grüne, schon früher erwähnte Haus,
das schon früher erwähnte, grüne Haus

English we have to say:

the green house mentioned earlier

What can we tell our students to make it easier for them to recognize and "un-
ngle" such German phrases? We know that the native German does not first determine
e beginning and the end of the extended adjectival phrase, then find the independent ad-
ctivals, then the "remaining elements" which make up the construction. Instead he reads
ght through such phrases. What are the signals which tip him off? No clear and unam-
guous rules can be given, but we can tell the student to watch out for prepositions and
rsonal pronouns which follow after articles or other determiners, e.g.

der von. . . .
ein uns. . . .
dieser vor. . . .

dverbs following determiners also frequently mark the presence of an extended adjec-
val phrase, e.g.

die noch. . . .
dieses ursprünglich. . . .

nce the student is aware of the presence of such a construction, the greatest difficulty
s been overcome. For decoding or deciphering extended adjectival phrases, he can fol-
w the steps which are outlined below. However, we should like to state emphatically
at the student simply has not learned to read German properly if he has to go through
is deciphering process. These are the steps to follow:

Identify   (1) the article or other determiner
           (2) the "independent" adjectivals which must precede the nom-
               inal in English
           (3) the nominal
           (4) the "other elements"

nese "other elements" should be either translated by a relative clause or by an extended
ljective construction which reverses the order of the parts in the German construction.
or example:

die häufigsten, durch Ausgrabungen hervorgerufenen, also nicht natürlich
bedingten Unfälle. . . .

(1) die : the

(2) häufigsten : most frequent

(3) Unfälle : accidents

(4) durch Ausgrabungen hervorgerufen, also nicht natürlich bedingt :
caused by excavations thus not conditioned by nature

the most frequent accidents which are caused by excavations and (which are
thus not conditioned by nature . . . [or] the most frequent accidents not condi
tioned by nature, but caused by excavations. . . .

We should perhaps add that the German sequence of adjectivals which modif
a nominal has a preferred order in much the same way that English has. Since our students rarely encounter difficulties in this respect we need not discuss it in detail. More
information on this point can be found in Seymour Chatman, "Pre-adjectivals in the Eng
lish nominal phrase," American Speech, XXV (1960), 83-100, and George K. Monroe, Ac
jectival Sequence in the German Nominal Phrase (unpubl. MA thesis; Brown University,
1961). The following two examples were taken from these sources:

not even almost all these many very fresh South Philadelphia buns. . . .

all die vier anderen runden braunen hölzernen Tische. . . .

(iii) NOMINALS modify verbals: kommt ⭠ (nächsten Montag) 'is coming ne
Monday,' kam ⭠ (eines Tages) 'came one (fine) day'; adjectival-adverbials: (meinem
Bruder) ➔ ähnlich 'similar to my brother,' (zwei Meter) ➔ hoch 'two meters high'; and
other nominals: Karls ➔ Buch 'Karl's book,' (das Buch) ⭠ (meines Bruders) 'my broth
er's book,' (eine Tasse) ➔ Kaffee 'a cup of coffee.'

Nominals modifying other nominals do not usually cause difficulties except
for instances illustrated by the last example where English structure leads students to
say things like *bringen Sie mir ein Glas von Bier! Generally, it is of little avail to the
student if we tell him that the German understands this to mean "a glass made out of
beer," but it may help to get the point across and set the basis for extensive drills on th
pattern: ein Teelöffel Zucker, 100 Gramm Käse, etc.

Difficulties often arise with phrases in which nominals modify verbals since
the student has no way of predicting the case in which the nominal is to appear. (Please
note that we are discussing only attributive modifiers here. Objective modifiers will be
treated in §3.2.) We have found it helpful to say that the nominal will usually appear in th
accusative case and to treat expressions in the genitive (which are much less frequent)
exceptions.

(iv) VERBALS in the infinitive and participle forms modify other verbals. I
finitives modify a considerable number of them: muss ⭠ sprechen 'must speak,' geht ⭠
einkaufen 'goes shopping,' lernt ⭠ singen 'learns to sing.' Participles on the other hand
modify only a very limited number of verbs, three of which are very common: hat ⭠
gesprochen 'has spoken,' 'spoke'; ist ⭠ gekommen 'has come,' 'came'; wird ⭠ gebroch
'gets broken.' (In other uses the participle is taken to be an adjective-adverb: gebrocher
Deutsch 'broken German,' spricht gebrochen 'speaks brokenly,' ist gebrochen 'is [alrea
broken.')

Since verb phrases in German differ considerably from the structure of Eng

sh verb phrases, they cause a good deal of trouble to the learner. We feel, therefore,
at they warrant detailed discussion which will point out the areas of conflict. Since they
e the most frequent, we will first discuss verb phrases which involve auxiliary con-
ructions, and then we will mention verb phrases in which no auxiliary constructions are
esent.

Auxiliary constructions.—In this discussion the full spellings are used in re-
rd to all English auxiliaries as cover symbols for all the forms with various stress re-
ctions and contractions, e.g. won't will appear as will not. Only when an auxiliary has
eaningful loud stress will there be any reference to stress conditions. The term "lexi-
l verb" is used for what is sometimes called "full verb, free verb, true verb," i.e. one
the thousands of verbs in the English and German lexica with an inherent semantic con-
nt and without a specifically grammatical function.

Perhaps we should add here a note of explanation as to why we consider aux-
ary constructions worthy of such detailed discussion. The main reason is that auxilia-
es are of the highest frequency in both English and German. Unless we introduce them
rly in our program of instruction, English-speaking learners will not be able to feel
atural" in German without dealing with meanings which in English are conveyed by the
odal auxiliaries. The conflicts which we encounter are even more fundamental with Eng-
sh do, have, be since our students have very pronounced grammatical habits of express-
g the important structural meanings of negation, interrogation, insistence, and echo-
bstitution via this small repertory of auxiliaries with special stress reductions and con-
actions. German operates in quite a different manner and this, as we all know, presents
grave learning problem, no matter how strongly we may feel about the "obvious" regu-
rity and reasonableness of the German auxiliary system. (In the description of the Eng-
sh verb auxiliaries we have greatly profited from W. F. Twaddell's monograph of this
le. Much of the description of German verb auxiliaries is based on the findings of the
ne Syntax of Substantive and Non-finite Satellites to the Finite Verb in German by M. H.
olsom [Ph.D. thesis; Cornell University, 1961; available on microfilm].)

Since our discussion must be based on English we follow the logical procedure
describing the grammatical behavior of the English auxiliaries, contrasting them with
eir German equivalents as we go along. In doing so we shall follow Twaddell's outline
osely.

3.11 THE "PRIMARY" AND THE "MODAL" AUXILIARIES

In English it is useful to distinguish two sets of auxiliaries: the "primary"
uxiliaries with subject-agreement -s and full Past syntax (have, be, do) and the "modal"
uxiliaries without -s and without full Past syntax (can, could, dare, may, might, must,
ed, ought, shall, should, will, would). In German it is also desirable to divide the auxil-
ries into two sets: the "modal" auxiliaries with identical forms in the 1st and 3d person
ngular present (sollen, wollen, dürfen, können, mögen, müssen) and the "primary" auxil-
ries which show a differentiation in the 1st and 3d person singular (sein, haben, werden).
rimary auxiliaries are more numerous in German than they are in English. Note that
oth German sets have a full Past syntax.

3.12 PRIMARY AUXILIARIES

Like many lexical verbs English <u>have</u> and <u>be</u> participate in a four-element system of constructions. The four formal elements are:

    I. PAST (-ed, -t, alternate stem, zero)
   II. CURRENT RELEVANCE (have + participle)
  III. LIMITED DURATION (be + -ing)
   IV. PASSIVE (be + participle)

Each of these four elements is called a "modification" by a special convention of regarding the past inflection, auxiliary + participle, or auxiliary + -ing as "modifying" the meaing of the lexical verb in the construction. Grammatically, these four modifications are potentially co-occurrent in all 16 possible combinations and limited only by the semanti compatibility of the lexical verb.

In the following paradigm, the arrangement is determined formally by runni through the combinatory possibilities.

(NO modification)

	eats	isst

(any ONE)

I	ate	ass, hat gegessen
II	has eaten	ass, hat gegessen, isst
III	is eating	isst
IV	is eaten	{ wird gegessen { ist gegessen

(any TWO)

I, II	had eaten	hatte gegessen
I, III	was eating	ass, hat gegessen
I, IV	was eaten	wurde (war) gegessen
II, III	has been eating	ass, hat gegessen, isst
II, IV	has been eaten	wurde gegessen, ist gegessen worden
III, IV	is being eaten	wird gegessen

(any THREE)

I, II, III	had been eating	hatte gegessen
I, II, IV	had been eaten	war gegessen worden
I, III, IV	was being eaten	wurde gegessen, ist gegessen worden
II, III, IV	has been being eaten	wurde gegessen, ist gegessen worden

(all FOUR)

| I, II, III, IV | had been being eaten | war gegessen worden |

A quick comparison of the two columns makes it clear that the two structure cannot be compared on a one-to-one basis, as any teacher of German has known all along But it should prove helpful to see just how these two systems are alike and how they diff

ey share the following features: The first component in a primary verb construction
ars the subject-agreement marker and/or the Past inflection. If no auxiliary is in-
lved, this first component is obviously the lexical verb. The potential co-occurrence
the four primary modifications is formally a grammatical principle of English, but it
s its semantic corollary: the meanings of the four modifications must be compatible.
nce these four modifications do not constitute a semantic system. Much of the difficul-
in describing the functions of English verb construction has arisen from attempts to
sign a meaning to the lack of one or more of the primary modifications. We must re-
ember that "present tense"—in both German and English—is a grammatical label, not
semantic description. Consider a clause, such as

er schwimmt täglich eine Stunde

course, we will go on calling this verb form a "present tense," but we must also re-
ember that its use in the above clause implies past and future meanings as well. Thus
can say that in both English and German a predicate without any of the primary modi-
ations is simply timeless—pure description, implicitly justified by a past record and
presumption of future continuation.

3.121 MODIFICATION I

Since this entire section of our study is concerned with PHRASES we will de-
te very little space to verb constructions in which only the first modification is applied
because such application involves the lexical verb only.

In English a construction containing the Past modification, with or without
her modifications, has either a limitation to the chronological past, or a focus upon non-
ality, or is automatic in "sequence of tenses."

3.1211 SEQUENCE OF TENSES

Let us consider the third function first, since English and German show com-
ete agreement in constructions which are syntactically dependent upon another construc-
on with Past modification:

he was there when I ___
er war schon da als ich ___

he blanks in the above frames can only be filled by verbs which show the Past modifica-
on (e.g. came, kam). There is no conflict since both languages demand this sequence of
nses. We should add, however, that German does have a degree of freedom which is
cking in English. Though it is quite generally considered inelegant, German speakers
uld complete the above frame with a verb involving the second modification, e.g.

er war schon da als ich gekommen bin

3.1212 LIMITATION TO CHRONOLOGICAL PAST

The first function of the Past modification implies a limitation to the chrono-
gical past.

he read a book

er las ein Buch = er hat ein Buch gelesen

It is evident from this example that German can express the meaning of the English exa‑
ple either by modification I or II. Many pages have been written about the differences be‑
tween these two German equivalents. We do not wish to enter into this discussion. For c
purposes suffice it to say that both versions occur and that they are interchangeable unc
most circumstances. We may add that hat . . . gelesen is more frequent in the South of *
German‑speaking area; that las occurs more frequently in writing expository prose or *
telling a story; that hat . . . gelesen is felt by most speakers to be more informal, collo‑
quial than las, more often used in everyday conversation (see also §6.3 ff.).

3.1213 UNCERTAINTY, UNREALITY, IMPROBABILITY

If an associated construction contains could, might, should, would, then "if"
Past modification signals uncertainty, unreality, improbability. For example: "If I had
enough money I could buy a new car." The meaning Contrary‑to‑fact is signaled by coul*
might, should, would + have + participle in an associated construction. For example: "If
had found out I would have gone immediately." In itself, the combined structure "If" +
Past modification . . . could, might, should, would is void of any time‑signaling content
and is compatible with contextual or situational clues specifying future, present, or past
chronology. As we all know, German differs most radically in regard to this third func‑
tion of the English Past modification: in all of these instances the German verb appears
in a form which we have called "general subjunctive." There is no need to describe the
forms here: any standard grammar book will do.

Our main difficulties as teachers of German arise from the fact that English
shows no difference of form whereas many German verbs do. To make students aware
that the English Past modification performs this extra function (which is devoid of any
time‑signaling content) we have found it useful to first show these two English sentences
side by side:

When I had enough money I bought a car

If I had enough money (today) I'd (would) buy a car

Explaining the matter in terms of this formula (if + Past . . . would, etc.) and such fram*
as cited has proved much more useful and less time‑consuming than a discussion of the
semantics of "conjecture, wish, improbability," etc. Once the students have grasped the
differences in function between the two had's we can tell them that German expresses th*
difference in form as well. As our next step we will contrast:

If I have enough money I'll (will) buy a car

If I had enough money I'd (would) buy a car

Only after we are sure that this contrast is clear to the student, after we have inserted
all kinds of time markers, e.g. today, this evening, tomorrow, etc., only then do we trans‑
pose our examples and show the same difference in German:

1) als ich genug Geld hatte, kaufte ich ein Auto

2) wenn ich genug Geld habe, kaufe ich ein Auto

[less frequently]: werde ich ein Auto kaufen

3) wenn ich genug Geld hätte, würde ich ein Auto kaufen

t this point the student will need a considerable number of drills, all using the frame:

wenn . . . . gen. subj., würde . . . . inf.

nly when this fundamental pattern is firmly established can we proceed to tell the stu-
ent about the freedom of arrangement which is found in modern colloquial German.

1) wenn er schneller ginge, würde er rechtzeitig kommen

2) wenn er schneller ginge, käme er rechtzeitig

3) wenn er schneller gehen würde, käme er rechtzeitig

4) wenn er schneller gehen würde, würde er rechtzeitig kommen

lthough most of our grammar books still tell us that only (2) is correct, we find that the
ther three versions occur more and more frequently. (4) is still felt by most Germans
ɔ be rather clumsy and should therefore be avoided. It is also true that the würde + inf.
hrase is more common with weak than with strong verbs since regular weak verbs do
ot have a distinctive form for the general subjunctive. It should be added that the wenn +
ifinitive + würde clauses are on the increase even in the language of modern literature
see Martin Tamsen, "Über 'wenn . . . würde' im modernen Deutsch," Deutschunterricht
ür Ausländer, IX [1959], 42-51) and our students should know about this for recognition
urposes. (We should continue our presentation of the general subjunctive by mentioning
hat wenn may be omitted [cf. §2.824] and that the main clause may be introduced by so
ɔr dann without change of meaning or word order, e.g. ginge or schneller, käme er recht-
eitig = ginge er schneller, so käme er rechtzeitig = ginge er schneller, dann käme er
echtzeitig [see also §6.11 ff.].)

3.122 MODIFICATION II: HAVE + PARTICIPLE

In English have + participle explicitly links an earlier event or state with the
urrent situation. Sometimes this means that an action which started in the chronological
ɔast is still going on at the present time or that its results are still evident at the present time. As Twaddell puts it: "It signals a significant persistence of results, a continued
ruth value, a valid present relevance of the effects of earlier events, the continued reli-
ability of conclusions based on earlier behavior." A sentence like "my family has lived
in this town since 1638" is a classic exemplification of this use of modification II.

German verb structure lacks such a means of combining past happenings with
present results. As we have seen in the preceding paragraphs the two modifications (Past
and haben/sein + participle) overlap in use and meaning. We might say that in this respect
the German tense system is more closely related to chronological time since whenever
we are confronted with the task of translating an English modification II into German we
have to ask ourselves something like "are they still doing it—is it still going on—what is
going on right now?" We might also put it another way: The German verb system seems
to stress the current relevance more than the fact that a given action or state had its be-

ginnings in the past. Let us compare these two sentences:

1) meine Familie wohnt seit 1638 in dieser Stadt
2) meine Familie hat seit 1638 in dieser Stadt gewohnt

As we all know the first sentence is the correct rendition of the English example which we cited above because the family is <u>still</u> living there. We can easily countercheck this translation by deleting the time expression, e.g.

1a) Meine Familie wohnt in dieser Stadt
'my family lives (is living) in this town'

By the same token our example (2) above does not tell us anything about the present whereabouts of the family—all it tells us is that the family started living there in 1638. If we omit the time expression we can easily see the difference:

2a) Meine Familie hat in dieser Stadt gewohnt = Meine Familie wohnte in dieser Stadt
'my family lived (has lived) in this town'

So far we have seen that an English modification II may be translated by a German present tense. Of course, this is not always the case—as the hypothetical questions which we listed above clearly indicate. In most instances, the English verb in modification II is translated by a German verb <u>either</u> in the Past modification <u>or</u> with modification II. (In regard to the choice between these two modifications, see §6.32.) In many cases this means that the German verb fails to convey shades of meaning given by the English verb in modification II. Compare these two sentences:

1) Four students have come out
2) Four students came out

The first sentence implies that they are still out, whereas the second one tells us nothing about their actions since they left. Both sentences may be translated by:

(1 + 2) Vier Studenten kamen heraus = Vier Studenten sind herausgekommen

Neither of the German equivalents tells us anything about the current whereabouts of the four students.

One of the problems which our students encounter when forming modification II in German is the choice between the auxiliaries <u>haben</u> and <u>sein</u>. It is clear that most verbs form the "perfect phrase" with <u>haben</u>. Also, we don't have much trouble in explaining that <u>sein</u> occurs with "verbs of motion," although the brighter students are quick to point out that most verbs signify some kind of motion. The best we can do is to list the most common "verbs of motion" such as <u>gehen</u>, <u>fahren</u>, <u>laufen</u>, <u>kommen</u> and to tell the students that it is this kind of motion which we mean. We have found that it is fairly easy to establish this semantic category of verbs—it is far more difficult to get the learner to remember it at the proper time. As we have found elsewhere, extensive drills are the only effective answer. The same is true for the other group of verbs which uses <u>sein</u> to form modification II: verbs of "inner change," e.g. <u>passieren</u>, <u>geschehen</u>, <u>sterben</u>, <u>einschlafen</u>. Then we must add that, by exception, the verbs <u>bleiben</u> and <u>sein</u> also belong here,

d by this time even the slower students have figured out that the semantic criteria for
r verb classification are vague at best. We have found it useful to admit frankly to our
udents that these criteria do not stand up under close scrutiny, that they are simply no
ore than convenient labels for a very limited number of German verbs which share this
ature of forming the modification II with the auxiliary sein. The only sure way of classi-
ing them is a complete list—labels like "verbs of motion" and "verbs of inner change"
ve been thought up for the convenience of the learner, not because the Germans make
e of any logical distinction between these two classes of verbs.

We must continue our discussion by mentioning that verbs which have a direct
ject (an object in the accusative case) always form modification II with haben, e.g.

>   er ist nach München gefahren
>   er hat meinen neuen VW gefahren

Although a text for beginners need make no mention of it, recent developments in German
nd to invalidate this statement. The feature as such is by no means new, but it is becom-
g more and more popular. Sentences like the following are no longer rare: wir sind neue
ege gegangen).

3.1221 CO-OCCURRENCE OF MODIFICATION I AND II

The form had + participle, the so-called pluperfect, signals that at some past
me a still earlier occurrence or state had a current relevance. Since the German plu-
erfect (the combination of modifications I and II) signals precisely the same thing, our
udents rarely have any trouble with this form, and we need not discuss it any further.

3.1222 MODIFICATION III: BE + -ING

This modification of the English verb is the most difficult to describe and the
ardest to learn for the non-native speaker of English. Rare indeed is the foreigner who
as mastered it. We should have to devote a good deal of space to this verb modification
this study were intended for speakers of German who wish to learn English. Fortunate-
y, we are directing our efforts to American students learning German, and thus we can
ell them that German simply lacks the distinction between "progressive form" and "sim-
le verb form," i.e. there is no German counterpart to the English modification III. What
e should do, however, is to draw a chart for our students, somewhat like this:

ich esse	= I eat	and	I'm eating
ich ass	= I ate	and	I was eating
ich habe gegessen	(I have eaten	and	I have been eating)
ich hatte gegessen	= I had eaten	and	(rarely) I had been eating, etc.

If matters rested here, our task would indeed be simple. It is, however, true
hat German is not entirely insensitive to the delicate semantic differences which modifi-
ation III exerts on some English verbs. But since an equivalent grammatical modifica-
ion is lacking, German must express these differences by other means, often by the in-
ertion of an adverbial, e.g. fast, beinahe:

1) she was dying with laughter
sie lachte sich fast, beinahe zu Tode

or by adding a stressed adverb to the verb: 101a (i)):

2) he stabbed his attacker
er erstach den Angreifer versus

he was stabbing his attacker
er stach auf den Angreifer ein

These are, of course, lexical differentiations replacing grammatical differentiations; we might say that the German verb is lexically modified. The third way in which German may express the semantic effects of modification III we should like to call lexical replacement i.e. an entirely different verb will be chosen in German. This third possibility is without doubt the most difficult because most of our dictionaries simply ignore this variation. Examples:

3) to think   denken, glauben, annehmen
   to be thinking   überlegen, nachdenken

   to fly   fliegen
   to be flying   wehen (im Winde)

   to feel   der Meinung sein, fühlen
   to be feeling   sich fühlen

   to look   schauen, blicken
   to be looking   aussehen

   to love   lieben
   to be loving   liebkosen, streicheln

3.123 MODIFICATION IV: *BE* + PARTICIPLE

This modification is, of course, the passive, and it has been semantically characterized thus: the subject referent undergoes an action or effect rather than (as often in constructions without modification IV) producing or constituting an action or state. It might be well to remind ourselves that the absence of this modification is by no means a denial of the semantics of passive meaning. Neither English nor German grammar has an "active voice"; "active" meaning is at most a by-product of the semantics of direct-object grammar. Thus, die Tür schliesst sich means fundamentally the same thing as die Tür wird geschlossen, although the grammatical constructions are quite different.

3.1231 *WERDEN* + PARTICIPLE

We all know, of course, that the German equivalent of modification IV is werden + participle:

a film is shown every evening
ein Film wird jeden Abend gezeigt

ost of our difficulties in teaching the passive stem from the dual nature of the participle. English as in German, the participle is at once part adjective and part verb. We can e its modifying nature in its ability to fulfil all the functions of the adjective; but it is rb-like in its ability to express tense (as we have seen) and voice and to be attended by bjects and objects. How does this dual nature of the particple express itself in the pasve modification? We can easily see that an English clause like

he was wounded

ambiguous. It may be the verb <u>wound</u> with modifications I and IV, and thus have a pasve meaning (in colloquial English: "he got wounded"). Or it may be just a form of the rb <u>be</u> (in modification I) plus a participle used as an adjective ("when I saw him, he was ounded," like "he was sick"). Similarly, a sentence like "the door is closed" may mean at someone is just closing it or that it is not open. In German this ambiguity is avoided the choice of the auxiliary: <u>er wurde verwundet</u> is a passive; <u>er war verwundet</u> is a rm of <u>sein</u> plus a participle used as an adjective. Also:

the door is closed → die Tür wird geschlossen
→ die Tür ist geschlossen

In helping our students to resolve this difficulty we have found it useful to tell em that the English verb phrase contains modification IV whenever they can insert the rm "being." Unfortunately, this handy rule of thumb works only in the present and past nses: in the perfect and pluperfect phrases the insertion of "being" tends to make the erb phrase so cumbersome as to conflict with the student's <u>Sprachgefühl</u>. (Our textbook riters have introduced various terms to mark this distinction. They speak of actional s. statal passives, or of passive-subject sentences vs. result-state sentences. The latter rms seem preferable, since the construction <u>ist . . . geschlossen</u> can be called a pasive only if we approach German in terms of the grammar of English.)

3.1232 PASSIVE CLAUSES WITH DATIVE OBJECT

There is a further peculiarity of English passives which tends to cause diffiulties when our students try to put it into German. We may consider all English passives s transforms of constructions not involving modification IV ("actives").

The war was won by the Allies ——→ the Allies won the war
[But] He was given a book ——→ *a book gave him
——→ a book was given to him
——→ ( ) gave him a book

n German the passive transforms of clauses involving verbs with a dative object retain his dative form in contrast to English:

man sagte <u>ihm</u>. . . . ——→ <u>ihm</u> wurde gesagt. . . .
they told <u>him</u> ——→ <u>he</u> was told

Unless we drill this pattern, the student will construct sentences like *er wurde ein Buch gegeben

which are incomprehensible to a German.

3.1233 OTHER PASSIVE AUXILIARIES

There are a number of German verbs aside from werden which are used in forming passives. Their use is still very limited—and should probably not be mentioned in a beginner's text—but their use seems to be on the increase. Their construction is very similar to the English pattern "he was given," e.g.

es wurde ihm gezeigt—er bekam es gezeigt	'he was shown it'
es wurde ihm geschenkt—er erhielt es geschenkt	'he got it as a gift'
es wurde ihm bezahlt—er kriegte es bezahlt	'he was paid for it'

Another pseudo-passive which is now used fairly frequently in German literature, although it was considered definitely substandard only a few decades ago, is the construction with gehören in the meaning of "ought to be":

er soll(te) befördert werden—er gehört befördert 'he ought to be promoted'

3.13 MODAL AUXILIARIES

In English there are four paired modals and four unpaired ones:

can	may	shall	will				
could	might	should	would	dare	must	need	ought

This pairing mainly shows up in the relationship of non-reality and sequence of tenses with /could/might/should/would which we have discussed and contrasted with German in section 3.1213. In addition, could occasionally functions as the Past partner of can.

English modals can therefore formally be divided into two classes. The major class will consist of the paired modals, the minor class of the unpaired ones. Within the minor class there is no unreal form and no differentiation for sequence of tenses. The minor class is also defective in varying degrees for various speakers today; some of the minor modals are passing into the category of catenatives (with following "to") and their former semantic function is taken over by other modals or catenatives. The modals do not co-occur, except in substandard speech. A phrase like "wouldn't dare to" is proof that dare is no longer a modal but has moved over into the class of catenatives.

The alternation of shall and will (should/would) is for some speakers determined by the traditional prescription in terms of the grammatical person of the subject. But the majority of speakers, particularly the younger people who are our students, do not adhere to this prescription. Instead they use shall almost exclusively in questions: shall then asks for instructions or suggestions as to future behavior, whereas will asks for pure prediction. E.g. What shall I do?; What will the neighbors think?

The relationship of need and must is similar: need asks for or asserts an opinion as to the contingent necessity or propriety of a specified behavior; must does not incorporate this element of contingency:

I <u>need</u> to go to faculty meetings

I <u>must</u> go to the next faculty meeting

3.131 DISTRIBUTION OF MODALS

The gradual decay of <u>dare</u> (we can henceforth omit <u>dare</u> from our discussion or two reasons: [1] its use as a modal is very limited among younger speakers, and [2] ts most common German equivalent <u>wagen</u> is not a modal at all, thus causing no interfer- nce in the patterning of the auxiliary verbs), <u>need</u>, <u>ought</u> is having its effects on the dis- ribution of English modals. From speaker to speaker there are some variations in usage ith and without "to" as between statement and question, affirmative or negative. Supple- ions are becoming more and more general, and some of these cause a great deal of diffi- ulty in learning German.

affirmative	negative
ought to	shouldn't
need to, must	don't have to
may	mustn't

n contrast to this, German here uses a regular pairing of negative and affirmative use:

sollen	ought to
nicht sollen	shouldn't
müssen	must
nicht müssen	don't have to
dürfen	may
nicht dürfen	mustn't

f we arrange the English-German equivalents in a somewhat different manner the points of conflict stand out clearly:

must	⟶	müssen
mustn't	⟶	nicht dürfen
may	⟶	dürfen
may not	⟶	{ vielleicht nicht [tun] / nicht dürfen

It is clear that <u>may not</u> presents a special problem. Unless we know the intonation, sen- tences like <u>he may not come</u> are ambiguous. They mean either non-permission or proba- bility of non-occurrence. In some cases this semantic ambiguity is resolved: "it may not rain" is clearly "vielleicht regnet es nicht." Fortunately, a change is taking place among younger speakers of English which resolves this ambiguity. Our students tend to substi- tute <u>might</u> for <u>may</u> when used as an appraisal of pragmatic contingency. They substitute <u>can</u> for <u>may</u> when used as authoritative permission. Note the strikingly parallel develop- ment among younger speakers of German:

(schätzungsweise) <u>dürfte</u> es heute nicht regnen

<u>kann</u> ich mit euch ins Kino gehen?

The semantics of _would_ is another special case. As a rule of thumb we can tell our students that _würde_ is the usual equivalent. This statement should be followed by an explanation that _würde haben_ and _würde sein_ 'would have, would be' very commonly are contracted to _hätte_ and _wäre_. _Would_, however, may also function as a past tense of _will_ and wherever so used it presents a grave problem of translation, e.g. "when we were in school we would play ball all afternoon" ➔ "als wir noch zur Schule gingen, spielten wir _regelmässig_ den ganzen Nachmittag Ball." Here the use of _would_ seems to describe a predictable and repeated kind of behavior in earlier time. But there are other uses of _would_, e.g. "at her trial Cavell would not tell a lie" ➔ "bei der Verhandlung _weigerte sich_ C. zu lügen." Here again _would_ seems to be the past tense partner of _will_. We have found it helpful to tell our students to insert _regelmässig_ if _would_ is substitutable by _used to_ (_pflegen_ + _zu_ infinitive is obsolete and should no longer be used in modern German) and to use _weiger_ + _zu_ + infinitive if _would not_ is substitutable by _refused to_.

We have discussed the main function of _could/might/should/would_ as conditionals when associated with constructions containing "IF" + Past modification, and their German corollaries (see §3.1213 above). These four modals also appear without an associated "if" construction: their meaning then is a lesser degree of urgency as to the pragmatic situation or a lesser degree of assurance as to probability. The German general subjunctive (see §3.1213) performs very similar functions and it tends to be used more frequently than its English equivalent. Our grammar books very often call this use the "subjunctive of politeness." E.g.,

whom could you recommend?   =   wen könnten Sie empfehlen?

We have based our discussion of the modal auxiliaries on the semantics of the English verbs without giving much space to the semantics of the German modal auxiliaries since most textbooks give adequate descriptions of their meanings. There is one feature, however, which is very often inadequately described in our beginning texts. The most common example of this peculiar feature follows:

you _should have bought_ aspirin—Sie _hätten_ Aspirin _kaufen sollen_

The student who is used to translating bit for bit will arrive at this German sentence:

Sie _sollten_ Aspirin _gekauft haben_

This is, of course, a perfectly good German sentence though it occurs less frequently than the construction with _hätte_ + infinitive + _sollen_. Its meaning, however, differs sharply from that which the student intended to convey:

you _were said to have bought_ aspirin

Compare the following examples and note their equivalents in English:

er kann gesprochen haben	he may/might have spoken
er hat sprechen können	he could/was able to speak
er kann den Brief geschrieben haben	he may have written the letter
er hat den Brief schreiben können	he was able to write the letter

er könnte gekommen sein	he might have come
er hätte kommen können	he could have come, he would have been able to come
er muss vorbeigegangen sein	he must have gone by
er hat vorbeigehen müssen	he was forced to go by

We have found that only extensive drills will familiarize the student with this German pattern. Lengthy grammatical or semantic explanations tend to be of no avail.

3.14 GRAMMATICAL CHARACTERISTICS OF AUXILIARIES

Quite apart from their versatile and subtle semantic functions, English auxiliaries, primary as well as modal, have certain grammatical features which are specifically peculiar to English grammar and thus cause a great deal of interference in the learning of German.

3.141 NEGATION

Auxiliaries occur before -n't (not) for sentence negation. If the sentence as a whole is to be negated it requires an auxiliary to precede the signal -n't or not; any other location of not specifically makes the negation partial, affecting part but not all of the sentence. For example: "He was working not for himself, not for his father, but for the company," "he was teaching biology, not biochemistry." The unstressed suffixed -n't is not only the normal negative signal with an auxiliary; it occurs only with auxiliaries (though rarely with may/might/shall) and the related copula "be" (but not with am).

As we all know, this feature causes a good deal of confusion to the learner of German: nicht is not restricted in its place of occurrence; on the contrary, its position in a sentence is one of the hardest features to define—aside from the added difficulty that auxiliary + -n't is very often rendered by kein- + substantival expression in German.

| I can't go | ich kann nicht gehen |
| I can't give you apples | ich kann Ihnen keine Äpfel geben |

The German "ich kann Ihnen nicht Äpfel geben" has a different stress and intonation pattern and corresponds to the English "I can give you not apples . . ." (on negation see also the sections on clauses, §2.90 and do, §3.142).

3.1411 INTERROGATION

Auxiliaries occur before the subject. The most common occasion for the sequence Auxiliary + subject is with interrogation. Except when the subject is the interrogative subject /who?/what?/which + nominal?/, English grammar demands an auxiliary before the subject in any question, whether affirmative or negative. There are other constructions with this sequence, but we will not discuss them here since they occur very infrequently (cf. Twaddell, English Verb Auxiliaries, p. 13). We have discussed the German equivalents of this grammatical feature of English in the section on clauses, cf. §2.7.

3.1412 STRESS AND PITCH SIGNALS

Another function of the auxiliaries is their occurrence as the place of gram-matical stress and pitch signals. Main stress on the auxiliary conveys the meaning of in-sistence on the truth value of the sentence as a whole, as against doubt or disagreement whether expressed or implied by the hearer or anticipated by the speaker as the hearer' probable attitude or reaction. German auxiliaries perform a similar function but only in-frequently. Instead, German tends to insert one of the emphatic adverbs, like <u>doch</u>, <u>wirk-lich</u>, <u>tatsächlich</u>, etc. In general, our students have no trouble with this function of Engli auxiliaries, except with <u>do</u> (see below).

3.1413 USE AS "ECHO"

Auxiliaries occur as the "echo" or substitute for the entire verb constructio and its complements in repetitions. This use of auxiliaries as echo-substitute is commo in answers to Yes-No-questions: "Will it rain?" — "No, it won't." Here once again Ger-man differs considerably from English patterns. If the auxiliary is repeated at all, Ger-man structure demands an <u>es</u> to serve as an object, e.g.

Barbara can read Hindi but Mac can't
Barbara kann Hindi lesen, aber Max kann <u>es</u> nicht
[More commonly]: . . ., aber Max nicht

Similarly, the example which we quoted above reads in German simply:

wird's regnen? — Nein.

The echo-substitute function is also found in the very frequent English question formula consisting of statement followed by tag-question: an auxiliary (+ -<u>n/t</u>) + pronoun subject. Fortunately, the German equivalent of this tag-question is invariable: it is always <u>nicht</u> (<u>wahr</u>)? The full formula <u>nicht wahr</u> sounds obsolete and/or pedantic and we should avoi teaching it to our teen-age students. Recently there has been an increasing tendency to replace <u>nicht</u> with a more emphatic and considerably less polite substitute: <u>oder</u>? For ex ample:

You are coming tomorrow, aren't you?
Sie kommen doch morgen, <u>oder</u>?
Sie kommen doch morgen, <u>nicht</u>?

3.142 ROLE OF DO

Let us now note that the grammatical role of <u>do</u> has become clear. <u>Do</u> is the semantically empty auxiliary, a grammatical dummy, which performs as auxiliary-qua-auxiliary in the four obligatory functions when no other auxiliary is semantically appro-priate in the construction. This also is the precise reason why our students have such dif ficulties with <u>do</u>: if its function is purely grammatical, if it does not "mean anything," the of course it is very hard to translate. It is easy to tell the students that there is no Ger-man counterpart for <u>do</u>, that there is no need in German verb grammar for such a gram-matical dummy. The student has deep-seated grammatical habits which cause him to

earch constantly for an equivalent for <u>do</u> when speaking German. We believe we can help
m by showing how <u>do</u> "fills in" for other auxiliaries and how German handles the same
ur functions without an auxiliary. Examples:

1)   Negation.

They <u>don't</u> work here	sie arbeiten nicht hier
He <u>didn't</u> come on time	er ist nicht rechtzeitig gekommen

2)   Interrogation.

<u>Did</u> you write a book?	haben Sie ein Buch geschrieben?
Where <u>does</u> she live now?	wo wohnt sie jetzt?

3)   Truth-value insistence.

<u>Do</u> come in!	Kommen Sie <u>doch</u> herein!
He <u>does</u> look silly!	er schaut <u>wirklich</u> blöd aus!

4)   Echo-substitute and tag-question.

Now it works, <u>doesn't</u> it?	jetzt geht's, nicht?
Hilde likes coffee but Herbert <u>doesn't</u>	Hilde trinkt gern Kaffee, aber Herbert nicht

ow that we have shown the student that German can function without the use of the "emp-
y auxiliary" <u>do</u>, we have to give him extensive drills to help him avoid these pitfalls.
There is no need to mention in an elementary text that <u>tun</u> does occasionally function as
uxiliary in modern German. In the standard language the dependent infinitive must invar-
ably take position one in the clause, e.g.

erfrieren tut hier keiner   'no one will freeze to death here.'

ll other uses of <u>tun</u> as an auxiliary are dialectal or substandard.)

3.10(b) ATTRIBUTIVE PHRASES

In contrast to the many areas of conflict which we have found and discussed
n the preceding paragraphs (3.10a) on ATTRIBUTIVE WORDS, we can quickly list the
arious kinds of ATTRIBUTIVE PHRASES since their structures are almost identical in
he two languages, and thus they pose little difficulty to the learner.

Two types of centerless phrases (see §3.4) also serve as attributive modifiers:

(i) PREPOSITIONAL PHRASES modify nearly all types of expressions, e.g.
erbals: <u>spricht</u> ← (<u>mit mir</u>) 'speaks with me'; nominals: <u>Geld</u> ← (<u>auf der Bank</u>) 'money
in the bank'; pronominals: <u>Sie</u> ← (<u>mit der Glatze</u>) 'you with the bald head'; adjectivals:
ein] (<u>mit der Grippe</u>) → <u>krankes</u> [Kind] '[a child] sick with the grippe'; and adverbials:
inks ← (<u>vom Bahnhof</u>) 'to the left of the station.'

(ii) CONJUNCTIONAL PHRASES modify adjectival-adverbials: (<u>so alt</u>) ←
(wie ich) 'as old as I,' älter ← (als ich) 'older than I.'

3.10(c) ATTRIBUTIVE CLAUSES

The special kinds of phrases called DEPENDENT CLAUSES (see §2.8) modif‹ nearly all types of expressions, e.g. verbals: kommt ← (wenn er Zeit hat) 'comes when he has time'; nominals: (der Mann) ← (der hier arbeitet) 'the man who works here'; pro‹ nominals: ich ← (der ich es getan habe) 'I who have done it'; adjectivals: (die neuen) ← (die ich gekauft habe) 'the new ones I bought'; and adverbials: drüben ← (wo er jetzt woh‹ 'over there where he lives now.'

| 3.2 | OBJECTIVE MODIFIERS |

So far in our discussion of phrase structure we have dealt with attributive modifiers only. We shall now take a closer look at the other type of modifier, OBJEC- TIVE MODIFIERS. Objective modifiers are pronominals or expressions for which pro- nominals can be substituted, i.e. expressions which can be replaced by pronominals. We will symbolize this relationship by writing: verbal ←o— object. For example, the phrase schreibt ←o— (jeden Brief) 'writes every letter' has the same structure as schreibt ←o— sie 'writes them.' On the other hand, the phrase schreibt ← (jeden Tag) 'writes every day' has the same structure as schreibt ← oft 'writes often.' Here we cannot sub- stitute a pronominal, but only an adverbial. It is therefore not an objective modifier but an attributive modifier of the type which we discussed in section 3.1. Objective modifiers are of two major types: certain clauses and words (alone or expanded).

3.21 CLAUSE OBJECTS

CLAUSE OBJECTS are either dependent clauses: weiss ←o— (wo er jetzt wohnt) '[I] know where he lives now'; sagt ←o— (dass er morgen kommt) 'says that he's coming tomorrow'; or in direct quotations, main clauses: sagt ←o— (ich komme morgen‹ 'says: "I'm coming tomorrow."'

We have discussed the various German clauses and how they differ from thei‹ English counterparts in sections 2.4-2.8.

3.22 WORD OBJECTS

WORD OBJECTS are always substantivals, either nominals: kennt ←o— (meinen Bruder) 'knows my brother'; pronominals: sieht ←o— mich 'sees me'; or adjec- tivals: kauft ←o— (die roten) 'buys the red ones.'

3.221 OBJECT AND CASE

Since English has exactly the same type of word-object construction, our stu- dents would encounter no difficulties in German if matters rested here. But we all know that German distinguishes between various objects according to case whereas English has no such distinction. English usage is adequately described by our formula:

$$\text{verbal} \leftarrow\text{o}\text{— object.}$$

German, on the other hand, the relationship looks somewhat like this:

```
                      ┌─ object in the accusative
        verbal ←o──── object in the dative
                      └─ object in the genitive
```

ince this is a distinction which is completely lacking in English, our students face im-
ense difficulties in making the correct choice in regard to the case in which the object
hould appear. Fortunately, the largest number of German words does take an object in
he accusative case (which is usually the student's first choice!), comparatively few take
n object in the dative case, and there are only a handful left which have an objective mod-
ier in the genitive case. For example:

ich sehe	←o—	den Mann
ich helfe	←o—	dem Mann
ich gedenke	←o—	des Mannes

'rom the very outset we must make it clear to the student that the case in which the ob-
ect appears depends on the verbal which we choose. It may be wise to abandon the term
transitive verb" since it only confuses the student with an English background. For him
here is no difference in "transitiveness" between

I see	←o—	him
I help	←o—	him
I remember	←o—	him

nstead, we should like to suggest a classification of verbs according to the case in which
he object appears. E.g. sehen would then be an accusative verb, helfen a dative verb, and
gedenken a genitive verb. Extensive drills will then help the student to distinguish the
hree classes of verbs.

3.222 DIRECT AND INDIRECT OBJECTS

In both English and German a verbal may have two objects: verbal + object +
object. Traditionally, we distinguish between a direct object and an indirect object. English structure differentiates these two by position, as we can easily demonstrate by using
nonsense words as objects:

1) I gave the tove the wabe
2) I gave the wabe the tove

In both examples the second object is the direct object, it symbolizes that which is being
given; whereas the first object is the indirect object standing for the person (or thing) to
whom it is given. If we compare with these two synonymous German sentences which follow we can imagine the difficulties of our beginning students:

1) ich gab der Frau das Buch
2) ich gab das Buch der Frau

In other words, German structure uses a totally different means, namely case, to indicate which substantival stands for the direct and which for the indirect object. Unless we

make this fundamental distinction clear to our students, they will always try to use position in determining which object is the direct one and vice versa.

A further characteristic of English structure tends to interfere with the lear-
ing of German object grammar. English can, in almost all instances, replace the indirec
object by a prepositional phrase. For example:

> verbal + object + object ~ verbal + object + prepositional phrase
> I gave him the book ~ I gave the book to him

This flexibility of English object grammar accounts for the many mistakes of the type:

> *ich gab das Buch <u>zu ihm</u>

Once again we must make it clear that this possibility is a peculiarity of English and that
it cannot be transferred to German. Extensive drills are needed to avoid this mistake.

We must also explain that this sequence of object + object holds true in German even if the direct object is a pronoun. In such cases English almost invariably uses
the alternate structure, i.e. the prepositional phrase. For example:

> (I gave the boy it) ⟶ I gave it <u>to the boy</u>
> ich gab es <u>dem Jungen</u>

When we teach translation into English we may use this distinction in formulating a rule
for our students, somewhat like this: if the direct object is a pronominal in German the
sentence in English will usually have the structure verbal + object + prepositional phrase

Although we cannot defend it on linguistic grounds (as we shall see in the following paragraphs), it has proved useful to beginners if we tell them that if a verbal has
two objects, the substantival which stands for the "person" will be in the dative and the
substantival which stands for the "thing" will be in the accusative. Needless to say, this
rule is not correct and its applicability is limited. Nevertheless, it does work in a good
many instances and thus helps the student to make fewer mistakes. As soon as his vocabulary increases and as he gets acquainted with those parts of German object grammar
which we are about to describe, the student will himself recognize the instances in which
our "rule" does not apply.

3.223 VARIETY IN OBJECT CASE

So far we have operated on the assumption that any German verbal which is
modified by two objects will have an accusative object and a dative object. We all know,
of course, that this is not true. As we have seen with simple object verbals, the relationships in English structure are much simpler than the German pattern:

> English: verbal ◂o— indirect object + direct object

> German: verbal ◂o— indirect object + { dative substantival
> accusative substantival
> genitive substantival

Once again, it will depend on the verbal whether the secondary substantival is in the dative, in the accusative, or in the genitive. There are a larger number of verbals which

ake accusative objects and dative objects. There is only one verb in German which is followed by two accusative objects: <u>lehren</u> 'teach.'

> er lehrte seinen Sohn die französische Sprache

More and more, however, one of the accusative objects is replaced by a dative object, and his development has now been accepted as standard practice (Duden, p. 453):

> er lehrte <u>seinem</u> Sohn die französische Sprache

But there is still a fair number of verbals which are modified by two substantivals in the accusative case. Our definition of an object (see §3.2) demands, however that an object be replaceable by a pronominal. In the case of all the verbals which we are about to discuss, only one of the substantivals in the accusative may be replaced by a pronoun, and the other accusative expression must therefore be considered an attributive modifier. (In English grammar such modifiers are sometimes called "objective complements.") Among these verbals are the so-called naming verbs, e.g. <u>nennen</u>, <u>taufen</u>, <u>heissen</u>, <u>titulieren</u>, <u>schelten</u>, <u>schmähen</u>, etc. They also include <u>fragen</u>, <u>bitten</u>, <u>finden</u>, <u>kosten</u>. A few examples follow:

> sie nannte mich einen garstigen Kerl
> ich muss dich etwas bitten
> er fragte mich schwierige Dinge
> ich finde Ihre Freundin eine sehr nette Person
> das Stück kostete mich im Grosshandel eine Mark

Verbals in which the second substantival is in the genitive case are very few and tend to be avoided altogether in the spoken language. They are still being extensively used in literature and our students should therefore know about them. These verbals include <u>erinnern</u>, <u>entheben</u>, <u>schämen</u>, <u>enthalten</u>, <u>erwehren</u>, <u>zeihen</u>, <u>bezichtigen</u>, etc. Again a few examples:

> ich bezichtigte ihn fälschlich des Ehebruchs
> ich habe ihn seines Amtes enthoben
> Karl konnte sich kaum des Lachens erwehren
> ich enthalte mich jeden Urteils
> er erinnerte sich jeder Einzelheit

In the spoken language such genitive attributes are frequently replaced by prepositional phrases, e.g.

> er erinnerte sich <u>an</u> jede Einzelheit
> ich schäme mich <u>wegen</u> seiner Eitelkeit, etc.

3.224 VERB + ZU + DATIVE

A number of English verbals with two objects cause a good deal of difficulty to the beginning student since their German equivalents involve an accusative object and a prepositional phrase (<u>zu</u> + dative).

they elected him president	sie wählten ihn <u>zum</u> Präsidenten
he was crowned emperor	er wurde <u>zum</u> Kaiser gekrönt
he made her a private secretary	er machte sie <u>zur</u> Chefsekretärin
they made him judge	sie bestellten ihn <u>zum</u> Richter

(Note: This presentation of German object grammer has necessarily been sketchy. For detailed account with many examples from modern German literature, see M. H. Folsom thesis.)

<table><tbody><tr><td>3.3</td></tr></tbody></table>

COORDINATE STRUCTURE: CENTER ⇆ CENTER

In a phrase such as <u>spricht</u> ←o— <u>Englisch</u> 'speaks English,' <u>Englisch</u> of course functions as the object of the verb <u>spricht</u>. If we expand this to <u>spricht</u> ←o— (<u>Englisch</u>, <u>Deutsch</u>, <u>Französisch</u>) 'speaks English, German, French,' we find that the phrase <u>Englisch</u>, <u>Deutsch</u>, <u>Französisch</u> performs the same function as the word <u>Englisch</u> that of object. But this time, no one of these three words modifies any of the others; each by itself can function as the object: <u>spricht</u> ←o— <u>Englisch</u>; <u>spricht</u> ←o— <u>Deutsch</u>; <u>spricht</u> ←o— <u>Französisch</u>. We therefore say that each one of these words is a center, and write <u>Englisch</u> ⇆ <u>Deutsch</u> ⇆ <u>Französisch</u> with an arrow pointing toward each center. In such a center ⇆ center construction, the last two centers are usually linked by a special class of word (coordinating conjunction) which performs only this function:

<u>Englisch</u> ← <u>und</u> → <u>Deutsch</u>; <u>Englisch</u> ⇆ <u>Deutsch</u> ← <u>und</u> → <u>Französisch</u>

Any two or more expressions which perform the same function may be linked in coordinate structure. In <u>Englisch</u> ← <u>und</u> → <u>Deutsch</u>, we have two coordinate words; in (<u>mit mir</u>) ← <u>oder</u> → (<u>mit Ihnen</u>) 'with me or with you,' we have two coordinate phrases; in (<u>er heisst Schmidt</u>) ← <u>aber</u> → (<u>ich heisse Meyer</u>) 'his name is Schmidt but my name is Meyer,' we have two coordinate clauses.

Since English structure treats coordinating conjunctions in this same way, our students have no difficulties with this aspect of phrase grammar and we need not discuss it any further.

We should add a note about punctuation. English orthography permits a comma after every member of a coordinate phrase. German orthography omits the comma before the last member if it is joined by <u>und</u>, e.g.

he speaks German, English, and French
er spricht Deutsch, Englisch und Französisch

On the other hand, German orthography requires a comma before <u>aber</u>, e.g.

his name is Schmidt but my name is Meyer
er heisst Schmidt, aber ich heisse Meyer

3.4 COORDINATE STRUCTURE: CENTER=CENTER (APPOSITION)

In the sentence Hans kommt 'Hans is coming,' Hans functions as the subject of kommt. If we expand this to mein Freund Hans kommt 'my friend Hans is coming,' we again find a phrase (mein Freund Hans) performing the same function as a word (Hans): that of the subject. And again, each part of the phrase can by itself perform the same function: Hans kommt; (mein → Freund) kommt. This is not, however, a center ⪤ center construction, because we cannot put a coordinating conjunction between the two parts of the expression. Saying mein Freund ← und → Hans requires us to change the verb from kommt to kommen and gives us a very different construction. The construction mein Freund Hans is customarily called one of APPOSITION. Since the two centers are identical with each other, we can write: (mein Freund) = Hans, putting an equal sign between them.

Only substantive expressions commonly stand in apposition with one another. Examples: Anna = (seine Schwester) 'Anna, his sister'; Sie = Dummkopf 'you nitwit'; ich = Idiot 'what a fool I am'; Sie = Ärmster 'you poor fellow' and also Paul = Meyer 'Paul Meyer,' Herr = Schmidt 'Mr. Schmidt,' Fräulein = Keller 'Miss Keller,' Dr. = Fischer 'Dr. Fischer.'

3.5 CENTERLESS STRUCTURE: X ←→ Y

The above three types of structure can all be regarded as examples of EXPANSION, in which each phrase as a whole still performs the same function as its center or centers. Quite different is the fourth type of structure, in which the phrase as a whole functions differently from either of its two parts. Here we shall write X ←→ Y with an arrow pointing both ways to indicate that there is no center. German (like English) has three types of centerless phrases.

3.51 PREPOSITION ←→ OBJECT

mit ←→ mir 'with me,' von ←→ hier 'from here,' in ←→ (einer Fabrik), 'in a factory,' zu ←→ sprechen 'to speak,' um ←→ (zu sprechen) 'in order to speak.'

Our students are well aware of the fact that the object of a preposition does not appear in the nominative case. Their difficulty with prepositional phrases in German stems from the fact that German has three cases in addition to the nominative in contrast to English which has only one. Any good textbook contains lists of the four groups of German prepositions, i.e.

preposition + accusative
preposition + dative
preposition + genitive (rarely used in the spoken language)
preposition + dative or accusative

The case it governs is part of the basic information about any given preposition and must be learned along with its lexical meaning. One of the syntactic functions of the inflectional forms then is simply to mark the linkage of a particular substantival to a given preposition. We all know by experience that it takes an extraordinary amount of time and a large number of specific drills before our students have learned this feature of German grammar, since no corresponding diversification exists in the structure of their native language.

3.52 SUBJECT ←—→ PREDICATE

er ←→ kommt 'he's coming,' (Mein Freund Hans) ←→ (spricht Englisch und Deutsch) 'my friend Hans speaks English and German.''

Since English structures identically, our students have no trouble with this feature of German grammar.

3.53 SUBORDINATING CONJUNCTION ←—→ SUBORDINATE CLAUSE

wenn ←→ (er morgen kommt) 'if he comes tomorrow,' dass ←→ (er kommen kann) 'that he can come,' weil ←→ (es so spät ist) 'because it's so late.'

The major kind of difficulty with this construction is caused by the word order within the subordinate clause. We have discussed this difficulty in the section on Clause Structure (cf. §2.8).

PARTS OF SPEECH | 4

4.0 | INTRODUCTORY

Our purpose in the present chapter is to examine the parts of speech of English and German and to see where differences exist which may give rise to conflicts. Before we begin our discussion, however, we need to be sure just what we mean by the "parts of speech" of a language. This is all the more necessary because our approach to this topic will be somewhat different from that of traditional grammar.

Traditional grammar assumes, for both English and German (and on the model of Latin), a total of eight different parts of speech. Two of these are defined in terms of meaning: (1) a noun is the name of a person, place, or thing; and (2) a verb is a word that makes an assertion or indicates an action or a state. Most of the remaining parts of speech are defined on quite a different basis, namely their function in relation to other words, especially to nouns and verbs. Thus (3) a pronoun is a word which stands for a noun; (4) an adjective is a word that modifies a noun or pronoun; (5) an adverb is a word that modifies verbs, adjectives, or other adverbs; (6) a preposition is a word that shows the relationship between its object and some other word; and (7) a conjunction is a word that connects words, phrases, or clauses. The final class of words, somewhat apart from the rest, is again defined on the basis of meaning: (8) an interjection is a word that expresses strong feeling or emotion.

Though the exact wording of these definitions is not always the same, the above formulations are more or less typical. It is important for us to examine these definitions in some detail, since they are the ones to which our students have been exposed—whether or not they have actually learned them.

The most extraordinary thing about these definitions is the fact that, in actual practice, we often do not follow them at all. For example, the word flight indicates an action and the word health indicates a state; according to the definitions, both of them would therefore seem to be verbs. But if one of our students calls them verbs, we will immediately correct him and say that they are not verbs but nouns. This is odd, since neither flight nor health is the name of a person, place, or thing. As another example, we call the word June in June is the time to plant corn a noun; and it can be replaced by the word now, as in Now is the time to plant corn. Following the definitions, one of our students may say that now, as a word which stands for a noun, must be a pronoun. If he does so, however, we will correct him and say that it is not a pronoun but an adverb—and this despite the fact that, in the above sentence, it does not modify a verb, an adjective, another adverb, or any kind of word at all.

49

What kind of information, lying outside the traditional definitions, do we rea_ ly use to decide whether a word is a noun, a verb, an adverb, etc.? A good way to find ou is to take a word which belongs to more than one part of speech and see how we determi what it is. Suppose, for example, that a student asks us: "Is the word dream a noun or a verb?" We are likely to give him some such answer as the following: "Do you mean a dream or to dream? If you mean a dream, then it's a noun; but if you mean to dream, then it's a verb." And here we have our answer. We do not really classify words as nour and verbs on the basis of their meanings. The noun dream is not a "thing," and the verb dream is not an "action," in any usual sense of these terms. Indeed, the meanings of words are totally irrelevant to their classifications. We classify words as nouns and verbs not on the basis of their meanings, but on the basis of (1) their form, (2) their func tion, and (3) certain words used with them which we can call "markers." This can be illu trated by taking a nonsense form such as gorb and examining it from these three points view:

1) Form. If we find that people say singular gorb and plural gorbs, we call gorb a noun. But if we find that they say 3d singular gorbs, past gorbed, past participle gorbed, present participle and gerund gorbing, we call gorb a verb.

2) Function. If we find that people use gorb as the subject of a verb ("Gorb tastes good") and as the object of a verb ("I hate gorb"), we call gorb a noun. But if we find that they use it as the center of a predicate ("We gorb it"), we call it a verb.

3) Markers. Such words as a/an, the, this, that mark gorb as a noun: a gorb the gorb, this gorb, that gorb. The word to marks gorb as a noun in some environments: turn to gorb, next to gorb, but as a verb in other environments: like to gorb, want to gorb

Form, function, and markers serve as the "clues" to the part of speech to which we assign a given word, whether we know its meaning or not. It should be empha- sized, however, that one of these factors alone may not be sufficient; we often need two, or even all three. An example of an ambiguous case, now famous because it has been cite so often, is given by C. C. Fries in The Structure of English (New York, 1952), p. 70:

Ship sails today.

Here the criterion of form fails us: ship can be either a noun or a verb. The criterion of function also fails us: ship can be either the subject of a verb or the center of a predicate The criterion of markers also fails us, since none are present. The word sails is equally ambiguous: it can be either a noun plural form, or a verb in the 3d person singular pres- ent. The only way we can remove these ambiguities is by adding a marker of some sort. If we add the word the in front of ship, all is clear: the ship sails. The marker the then identifies ship as a noun, and function identifies sails as a verb. If we add the after the word ship, all is again clear: ship the sails. The marker the identifies sails as a noun, and function identifies ship as a verb.

4.1 FORM, FUNCTION, MARKERS

The use of form, function, and markers to identify parts of speech can be nicely illustrated by such nonsense poems as the following:

Jabberwocky

'Twas <u>brillig</u>, and the <u>slithy toves</u>
Did <u>gyre</u> and <u>gimble</u> in the <u>wabe</u>;
All <u>mimsy</u> were the <u>borogoves</u>,
And the <u>mome raths outgrabe</u>.
— Lewis Carroll

Gruselett

Der <u>Flügelflagel gaustert</u>
durchs <u>Wiruwaruwolz</u>
die rote <u>Fingur plaustert</u>
und grausig <u>gutzt</u> der <u>Golz</u>.
—Christian Morgenstern

Most people feel quite confident about classifying the underlined words in Jabberwocky as either nouns, verbs, or adjectives; and of classifying those in Gruselett as either nouns or verbs. (It is obvious that Morgenstern also knew how to make this classification in German: he apparently had no trouble in deciding which words, as nouns, should be written with a capital letter, and which words, as verbs, should be written with a small letter.) Since we do not know the meanings of any of these underlined words, it is obvious that their meanings are irrelevant to our classification of them. Indeed, it is only <u>after</u> we have decided whether one of the nonsense words is a noun or a verb that it takes on a certain meaning. We then have a vague feeling (as Alice said: "It seems to fill my head with ideas—only I don't exactly know what they are!") that each of the nouns means some sort of thing (or perhaps animal) and that each of the verbs means some sort of action. These, however, are not meanings in the usual referential sense, but rather "class meanings" or "structural meanings." The vague meaning "thing" is part of the class meaning of all nouns, and the vague meaning "action" is part of the class meaning of all verbs.

It is useful to repeat each of these poems and, by replacing the nonsense forms by numbers or letters, to reveal the various structural devices which enable us to classify them according to part of speech. For good measure, we also replace the stems of the German words <u>rote</u> and <u>grausig</u>. The two poems then appear, structurally, as follows:

Jabberwocky

'Twas ___1___, and the __2__y __3_s
Did _4__ and __5___ in the _6__;
All _7__y were the ___8____s,
And the _9__ _10_s out_11___.

Gruselett

Der _____A_____ ___B__t
durchs _____C_____,
die _D_e __E___ ___F___t
und __G_ig _H__t der _J__.

Though it would be interesting to investigate <u>all</u> the structural clues revealed in the skeleton forms of the two poems, we must limit ourselves to just a few remarks.

In Jabberwocky, word ___1___ is ambiguous. Most people classify it as an adjective, on the model "'twas peaceful" etc.; but this same slot can also be filled by a noun, e.g. "'twas summer." Words __2__y and _3__s, however, are clear. Word _3__s is marked as a noun by form (noun plural ending -<u>s</u>), by function (subject of the verb phrase "did _4__ and __5___"), and by the marker <u>the</u>. Once this identification is made, word _2___y is marked as an adjective by form (the suffix -y, as in slimy, greasy) and by function (noun modifier), in which the marker the also plays a part.

In Gruselett, word _____A_____ is marked as a noun by function (subject of the verb ___B___t) and by the marker der; the combination of these two clues also tells that _____A_____ is a masculine noun and that it is in the nominative singular. Word ___B___t is marked as a verb by form (3d person singular present ending -t) and by function (center of the predicate ___B___t durchs _____C_____). Word _____C_____ is marked as a noun by function (object of the preposition durch, which is also a marker) and by the marker s, short for das, both of which clues tell us that _____C_____ is neuter singular and in the accusative case.

These nonsense poems show that the total lexicon (i.e. the total list of all words) of English and of German falls rather clearly into two different types of words. Words which can be replaced by nonsense forms, or even by numbers or letters or blank are CONTENT WORDS. Those which we must leave in, in order to show the necessary grammatical structure, are FUNCTION WORDS. Content words are said to have LEXICA MEANING, i.e. meaning in the usual sense of that term; function words are said to have STRUCTURAL MEANING. These terms are relative. Content words all have some structural meaning, namely the class meaning of the part of speech to which they belong. It is this structural meaning which persuades us to say that a dream is in some vague way a "thing" and that to dream is in some vague say an "action." Function words usually have a certain amount of lexical meaning, though it can be very slight or even non-existent. For example, the to of English to dream, and the zu of German zu träumen, seem to have no lexical meaning at all, but only structural meaning.

4.2 | CONTENT WORDS AND FUNCTION WORDS

If we examine the lexicons of English and German from this point of view, we find the following:

1) Content words. Each language has only a few classes of content words. We shall classify the content words of English into nouns, verbs, adjectives, and adverbs (though most of the adverbs are derived from adjectives); and we shall divide the content words of German into nouns, verbs, and adjective-adverbs. Though these classes are ver few in number, they are enormous in size. Not only does each class have thousands and thousands of members, but each of them is also an "open" class, i.e. the language is so constructed that new members can easily be made up. This process goes on all the time, either through borrowing (sputnik, snorkel), through new creation (goof, finalize), or through a combination of the two (nylon, astronaut).

2) Function words. Each language has a relatively small group of function words, numbering only a few score. Furthermore, they form "closed" classes, since such words as pronouns, prepositions, and conjunctions are not readily created or borrowed. Just how many classes of function words there are depends on how far we want to go in our classification. English and German have easily definable classes of pronouns, deter-

ners, prepositions, coordinators, and subordinators—though there is some overlap be-
een them (e.g. English <u>since</u>, German <u>seit</u> are both prepositions and subordinators). But
class traditionally called "adverb" (excluding those adverbs which are content words)
little more than a catchall, into which we put words which do not fit into any of the oth-
classes. This is perhaps a good solution, however, since it allows us to set up what-
er subclasses of adverbs we find useful.

We are now ready to examine the various parts of speech of English and Ger-
n and to discuss the similarities and differences between the two languages. We shall
gin with the content words, continue with the easily definable classes of function words,
l end with a discussion of the infinitely classifiable adverbs.

4.3 NOUNS

Nouns are marked by function in much the same way in both English and Ger-
n. They serve as subjects of verbs, as objects of verbs, as objects of prepositions, as
ms modified by adjectives and determiners, as subjective complements ("they are <u>stu-</u>
<u>its</u>" like "sie sind <u>Studenten</u>"), and as fillers of certain other slots occupied also by ad-
rbs ("is coming <u>next Tuesday</u>" like "kommt <u>nächsten Dienstag</u>" vs. "is coming <u>now</u>" like
ommt <u>jetzt</u>"). A striking difference between the two languages is the fact that English
ins function freely as modifiers of other nouns: <u>kitchen table</u>, <u>atom bomb</u>, whereas the
rresponding expressions in German are compound nouns: <u>Küchentisch</u>, <u>Atombombe</u>.

English and German nouns are marked as such by comparable sets of deter-
ners: <u>the spoon</u> like <u>der Löffel</u>, <u>this knife</u> like <u>dieses Messer</u>, <u>my fork</u> like <u>meine Ga-</u>
l, <u>which plates</u> like <u>welche Teller</u>. The two languages differ, however, in the fact that
ch markers signal case and number in German, whereas they do not do so in English
cept for <u>this/these</u>, <u>that/those</u>, which signal number in English). These matters will
discussed in more detail in the sections on compulsory categories.

English and German nouns are marked as such by large numbers of deriva-
nal suffixes. In part they are similar in the two languages: <u>(work)er</u> like <u>(Arbeit)er</u>,
en)ing like <u>(Öffn)ung</u>, <u>(child)hood</u> like <u>(Kind)heit</u>, <u>(friend)ship</u> like <u>(Freund)schaft</u>, <u>(king)-</u>
m like <u>(König)tum</u>, <u>(reac)tion</u> like <u>(Reak)tion</u>, <u>(real)ity</u> like <u>(Real)ität</u>, etc. In part, how-
er, the affixes are quite different. German has nothing like the English contrast between
ins in /s/ (<u>the advice</u>, <u>the house</u>, <u>the use</u>) vs. verbs in /z/ (<u>to advise</u>, <u>to house</u>, <u>to use</u>).
glish has nothing like the German affix <u>Ge-</u> in Gebüsch (beside <u>Busch</u>), Gebrüder (be-
le <u>Bruder</u>), etc. English has a diminutive suffix /-i/, but it is used only with words re-
ring to persons (<u>Mummie</u>, <u>Billy</u>) and to small animals, especially pets (<u>birdie</u>, <u>doggie</u>,
ty); German has two diminutive suffixes, <u>-chen</u> and <u>-lein</u>, which can be used with many
es of nouns (<u>Häuschen</u>, <u>Tischlein</u>), plus a suffix <u>-i</u> used with words referring to persons
api, <u>Mutti</u>, <u>Bubi</u>). A full discussion of noun affixes would go far beyond the aim of this
apter. We need to note here merely that the marking of words as nouns through the pres-
ce of various affixes is a feature common to both languages.

English and German nouns are marked as such by inflection for case and number, but in drastically different ways. The English system can be illustrated as follows

Singular,	general	boy	/'bɔi/	sheep	wife	man
	possessive	boy's	/'bɔiz/	sheep's	wife's	man's
Plural,	general	boys	/'bɔiz/	sheep	wives	men
	possessive	boys'	/'bɔiz/	sheep's	wives'	men's

The vast majority of English nouns are inflected like <u>boy</u> and show only two different pl nemic shapes for these four grammatical forms. A few words like <u>sheep</u> also show two different phonemic shapes, but in a different distribution. Another small group, like <u>wi</u> shows three different shapes. Still another small group, like <u>man</u>, shows four different phonemic shapes. Only on the basis of this last group are we justified in setting up four grammatically different forms.

The German system of inflection for case and number can be illustrated by the following examples:

Sing.	nom.	Wagen	Frau	Knabe	Name	Mutter	Vater	Sohn
	acc.	Wagen	Frau	Knaben	Namen	Mutter	Vater	Sohn
	dat.	Wagen	Frau	Knaben	Namen	Mutter	Vater	Sohn(e
	gen.	Wagens	Frau	Knaben	Namens	Mutter	Vaters	Sohn(e
Plural		Wagen	Frauen	Knaben	Namen	Mütter	Väter	Söhne
	dat.	Wagen	Frauen	Knaben	Namen	Müttern	Vätern	Söhne

Some nouns, like <u>Wagen</u>, <u>Frau</u>, <u>Knabe</u>, show only two different forms, though in differe distributions. Others, like <u>Name</u> and <u>Mutter</u>, show three different forms, again in diffe ent distributions (the distribution of the three forms is still different in <u>Herz</u>). Still oth ers, like <u>Vater</u>, show four different forms. The maximum number of different forms is four or five, as illustrated by <u>Sohn</u>. It is worth noting that no one type of noun shows m than three different forms in the singular; only the different distributions of these form justify us in setting up four different noun cases in the singular. The above classes of nouns never show more than two different forms in the plural; and even noun modifiers never show more than three different forms in the plural, since the nominative and the accusative are always identical.

A type of noun not shown in the above table can be illustrated by the words <u>Beamt-</u> (<u>der Beamte</u>, <u>ein Beamter</u>, <u>die Beamten</u>, <u>zwei Beamte</u>) and <u>Gut-</u> (<u>das Gute</u>, <u>viel Gutes</u>). Such nouns take adjective endings, and hence show two different forms in most cases. They differ from adjectives in that they take endings when they are subjective complements; contrast <u>er war Gefangener</u> vs. <u>er war gefangen</u>.

In the section on compulsory grammatical categories it will be pointed out that students are quite unprepared for the four cases of German nouns, since English has at the most two cases and the English possessive is in many ways different from th German genitive. Students are, on the other hand, quite familiar with inflection for num ber, since this category is just as compulsory in English as it is in German. The confli which arises is not in the category as such, but rather in the very different form it take in the two languages. Aside from a few forms like <u>foot—feet</u>, <u>mouse—mice</u>, <u>man—men</u>,

-oxen, and learned plurals like criterion—criteria, alumnus—alumni, English has only
ingle type of noun plural formation, consisting of the following three shapes in comple-
ntary distribution:

$$/-\text{ịz} \sim -s \sim -z/,$$

nely /-ịz/ after stems in /s z š ž č ǰ/ (pass—passes, rose—roses, bush—bushes, ga-
e—garages, patch—patches, badge—badges), /-s/ after all other voiceless phonemes
ǫ—caps, cat—cats, pack—packs, cliff—cliffs, myth—myths), and /-z/ after all other
ced phonemes (cab—cabs, road—roads, bag—bags, cave—caves, tithe—tithes, bell—
ls, bone—bones, key—keys, etc.).

In contrast to this, even aside from such forms as Doktor—Doktoren (with
ess shift) and such learned plurals as Atlas—Atlanten, Thema—Themata, German has
less than six different plural types. Furthermore, five of these six types have two
pes each, in complementary distribution, as follows:

1) — ~ -e, namely—after stems in -e, -el, -en, -er, and the diminutive suf-
es -chen and -lein (Gebäude—Gebäude, Mittel—Mittel, Wagen—Wagen, Zimmer—Zim-
r, Hündchen—Hündchen, Schifflein—Schifflein), but -e otherwise (Tag—Tage, Jahr—
re, etc.).

2) ⸚ ~ ⸚e, namely ⸚ after stems in -el, -en, -er (Mantel—Mäntel, Garten—
·ten, Vater—Väter), but ⸚e otherwise (Gast—Gäste, Sohn—Söhne, Hut—Hüte, etc.).

3) ⸚er ~ -er, namely ⸚er after stems with umlautable vowels (Blatt—Blätter,
·f—Dörfer, Buch—Bücher, Haus—Häuser), but -er otherwise (Lied—Lieder, Brett—
·tter, etc.).

4) -n ~ -en, namely -n after stems in -e, -el, -er (Blume—Blumen, Dattel—
·teln, Feder—Federn), but -en otherwise (Frau—Frauen, Graf—Grafen, etc.).

5) -s, as in Kino—Kinos, Hotel—Hotels.

6) -e or -en in adjectival nouns, e.g. zwei Beamte but die Beamten, zwei Be-
·nte but meine Bekannten, etc.

The teaching problem which these German plural types present can perhaps
described as follows. From their English, students have become accustomed to form-
nearly all plurals in a single way, namely by adding /-ịz ~ -s ~ -z/; in German they
st learn to form the plural in any one of six different ways, only one of which is by add-
-s. But not even this is the whole story. The single plural ending in English has three
erent shapes; since they are in complementary distribution, the choice between them
automatic and students are generally not even aware of the differences between them.
e of the six German plural formations have two shapes in complementary distribution.
· choice between the shapes within each type is automatic for a native speaker of Ger-
·n, but certainly not for a foreign learner, who must learn their complementary distri-
ion at the same time that he learns the six basic types. To complicate the problem still
·ther, the complementary distribution within the types numbered (1) through (4) above is
·nologically determined (i.e. determined by the phonemic shape of the stem), whereas
·complementary distribution within type (6) is syntactically determined (i.e. determined
·whether or not the noun is preceded by a particular class of determiner).

There is no way in which the plural formation of German nouns can be mad easy. The best we can tell our students is that, after they have learned the commonest one thousand nouns or so, they will find that most other masculines and neuters add -e and most other feminines -(e)n. This is small comfort to a student who is just starting learn the commonest one thousand. For him the only answer is: learn the plural along with the singular and the gender of each noun, i.e. learn not simply <u>Bruder</u>, but <u>der Br</u> der, plural <u>Brüder</u>.

4.4 VERBS

Verbs are marked by function in much the same way in both English and Ge man. They serve as the center of the predicate, and they can take objects: "he <u>gave</u> me book" like "er <u>gab</u> mir ein Buch." English and German verbs are most clearly marked such by inflection for tense and mood though the latter is very restricted in English (se §6.11).

he gives   :   he gave

er gibt   :   er gab

Our languages differ considerably in the ways in which they use the various verb forms and some of these differences give rise to conflicts. Students are quite unprepared for applications of the German subjunctives and for the strikingly different meanings of the past tenses in English and German. On the other hand, students are familiar with inflec tion for person/number though the many different forms of German verbs present a gr learning problem. Once again, the conflict which arises is not in the part of speech as such, but rather in the very different forms which it takes in the two languages. Areas conflict (e.g. subjunctives, past tenses, participles) will be described and discussed in tail in the sections on compulsory categories. The following tables are merely intended show where such conflicts are likely to arise.

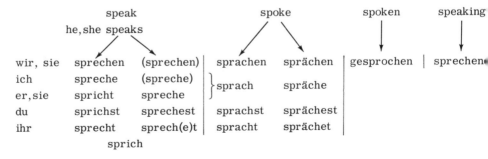

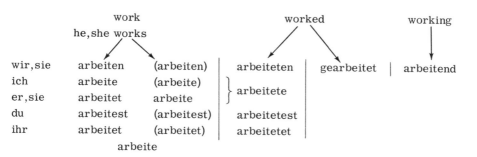

4.5 | ADJECTIVE-ADVERBS

In both English and German adjectives are marked by function in much the
[sa]me way: they are used to modify nouns ("hot coffee" = "heisser Kaffee"). The most
[str]iking difference between adjectives in the two languages is the fact that German adjec-
[tiv]es inflect for case, number, and gender in attributive position. The concepts of case
[and] gender and the difficulties they present to the student will be discussed in the section
[on] compulsory grammatical categories. To further complicate matters, German adjec-
[tiv]es have two sets of endings (commonly called "strong" and "weak") depending on the
[typ]e of determiner which precedes the adjective. In both languages, adjectives are further
[cha]racterized by inflection for comparison. English has two means of comparison: the ad-
[dit]ion of the endings -er and -est (this is sometimes called the synthetic method, e.g.
[pre]tty, prettier, prettiest), and the use of the function words more and most (this is called
[the] analytic method, e.g. beautiful, more beautiful, most beautiful). In sharp contrast to
[thi]s, German compares all adjectives by adding the endings -er and -st, e.g. schön,
[sch]öner, schönst-. The structure of German allows us to set up a group of content words
[wh]ich we have called adjective-adverbs. We can do this because predicative adjectives
[and] the corresponding adverbs are always identical in form. In English, on the other hand,
[we] have to set up two different groups of content words: adjectives of the type quick, beau-
[tif]ul, essential and adverbs of the type quickly, beautifully, essentially. There is, however,
[a s]mall number of adverbs in English which is identical in form with the corresponding ad-
[jec]tives, e.g. fast, late, hard, near, early. Although this closed subclass comprises only a
[few] words it is very important to us as teachers of German since it affords us a valuable
[me]ans of comparison:

English:	quick-ly	(open class)	fast	(closed class)
German:	-		schnell	(open class)

4.51 CONFLICTS

The conflicts which give rise to students' errors can be described under three
[he]adings: (1) endings, (2) comparison, and (3) predicative and adverbial use. Let us first
[ex]amine the third area since it gives us a good starting point for the other two. The first
[dis]tinction which we have to establish in the minds of our students is that between attrib-

utive and predicative use of adjectives. English shows no distinction between these two
uses; as a consequence our students often have trouble keeping them apart:

the car is <u>fast</u>   like   the <u>fast</u> car

As we all know, German adjectives behave in a very different way:

der Wagen ist <u>schnell</u>   unlike   der <u>schnelle</u> Wagen

Many of our beginners fail to see that German adjectives inflect for case,
number, and gender in attributive position only. This erroneous assumption leads to mi
takes of the type

*das Mädchen ist <u>hübsches</u>

To emphasize the different behavior of adjective-adverbs in the two languages, we have
found it useful to contrast them as follows:

the | beautiful | girl   das <u>schöne</u> Mädchen

the girl is | beautiful | das Mädchen ist | schön |

the girl sings <u>beautifully</u>   das Mädchen singt | schön |

Contrasting sets like these quickly drive home the point that English shows identical
forms for attributive and predicative adjectives, but a different form for the adverb,
whereas German shows identical forms for predicative adjectives and adverbs, but a dif
ferent form (or rather different forms) for the attributive adjective.

The major area of conflict concerns the various endings of German attributive adjectives. If our object is (as it should be) the automatic selection of the correct ad
jective ending when speaking German, then a listing of these various endings in a set of
tables is of little help. The student will memorize the table, and with a little prodding wi
be able to recite such a table quickly and correctly, but he will not be able to use indivi
ual forms correctly in conversation. Only an enormous amount of drilling with pattern
sentences will bring about the desired result. Unless we continue such drills throughout
the semester, our students will quickly forget the adjective endings. Therefore we have
found it helpful to include attributive adjectives in all drills following the presentation o
adjectives.

The third area which leads to conflicts concerns the comparison of adjective
adverbs. English uses the synthetic method of comparison most often for one-syllable ad
jectives: <u>large</u>, <u>larger</u>, <u>largest</u>, although a considerable number of polysyllabic adjective
may also be compared in this way, e.g. <u>holier</u>, <u>shallowest</u>, <u>nobler</u>, etc. Most polysyllabi
adjectives, however, are compared analytically. German, on the other hand, compares a
adjective-adverbs regardless of syllable count synthetically, i.e. by adding the endings
<u>-er</u> and <u>-st</u>.

der andere Hut ist <u>hübscher</u>

der <u>schönste</u> Tag meines Lebens

From what we know about the behavior of English adjectives, we do not expect difficultie

one-syllable forms like <u>hübsch</u>, <u>schön</u>, etc. But adjectives like <u>beweglich</u>, <u>sparsam</u>, <u>cher</u>, etc. tempt the beginner to compare them analytically, leading to mistakes of type:

*mein Vater ist <u>mehr sparsam</u> als meine Mutter

this reason we have found it helpful to build our drills for adjective comparison und polysyllabic forms.

A special effort must be made to acquaint the student with the fact that all applies to adverbs as well, because of such English patterns as <u>slow</u>, <u>slower</u>, <u>slow-</u> but <u>slowly</u>, <u>more slowly</u>, <u>most slowly</u>. For example:

die Strassenbahn ist <u>langsamer</u> als der Bus
der Bus fährt <u>langsamer</u> als die U-Bahn

German, superlative adjective-adverbs are rarely used without endings:

das ist ja <u>höchst</u> interessant

ch more commonly, inflected forms are used instead:

predicative: Peter ist <u>der jüngste</u>   or
              Peter ist <u>am jüngsten</u>

adverb: Hilde machte es <u>am geschicktesten</u>
              dort kauft man <u>am billigsten</u> ein

ce no comparable prepositional phrase exists in English, special drills are needed to ke the student familiar with this feature of German superlative adjectives.

A few German adjective-adverbs have special predicative-adverbial forms t add <u>-s</u> to the stems. Compare these examples:

die schöne Lage   :   die Lage war schön
die andere Lage   :   die Lage war ander<u>s</u>

e commonest members of this group are:

ander-	besonder-	recht-	link-	stet-
anders	besonders	rechts	links	stets

Another feature of German adjectives is likely to cause trouble to our begin-ng students since it is almost unmatched by a comparable feature in English. English ucture allows us to say things like:

the idle rich
the poor
the blind

te that all these phrases are plurals, i.e. if they function as subjects of clauses the rbs in these clauses appear in the plural form. If we wish to use a singular, however, have to insert the "noun" <u>one</u>. For example:

I take the green <u>one</u>
give me a larger <u>one</u>

Such phrases, i.e. determiner + adjective + <u>one</u>, may also form plurals:

> an old turkey is fine but young <u>ones</u> are better
> the slow <u>ones</u> won't make it

In contrast to this, German adjectives can occur freely after determiners and without a noun following. When so used their gender and number is determined by their antecedent. That is to say, a statement like "I'll take the green one" must be rendered either as

> ich nehme <u>den grünen</u>   or
> ich nehme <u>die grüne</u>   or
> ich nehme <u>das grüne</u>

Drills for this feature of German adjectives can easily be constructed in frames like these:

> Ihr Anzug ist nicht <u>der richtige</u> für dieses Wetter
> Ihre Mütze ist nicht <u>die richtige</u> für dieses Wetter
> Ihr Kleid ist nicht <u>das richtige</u> für dieses Wetter
> Ihre Handschuhe sind nicht <u>die richtigen</u> für dieses Wetter

> Packen Sie sich doch <u>einen wärmeren</u> ein
> Packen Sie sich doch <u>eine wärmere</u> ein
> Packen Sie sich doch <u>ein wärmeres</u> ein
> Packen Sie sich doch <u>wärmere</u> ein

4.6 FUNCTION WORDS

Our discussion of the function words in our two languages can be brief since the differences which exist are few. In general it can be said that our students encounter difficulties, not so much in the definition and function of these parts of speech, but rather in the use and application of the morphological changes which some of the function words undergo, or which they cause other words to undergo when they are modified by these function words. Thus we can say that our major teaching effort must be directed at drilling the forms of German <u>pronouns</u> and <u>determiners</u>. Once the students have mastered these forms and are thoroughly familiar with the concepts of case, number, and gender (see Section 5) they encounter little difficulty in their use.

4.61 CONJUNCTIONS

In English we hardly ever have occasion to subdivide a group of function words generally called <u>conjunctions</u>. English conjunctions can, of course, be subdivided by structural criteria, and it has proved useful to demonstrate to our students the different behavior of subordinators (e.g. <u>because</u>) and coordinators (e.g. <u>for</u>). For example:

> I could easily spot him <u>for</u> he was wearing a white suit
> I could easily spot him <u>because</u> he was wearing a white suit

ere the two conjunctions occupy the same slot, namely the position between clauses.
owever, while we can transpose the second example

> Because he was wearing a white suit I could easily spot him

e cannot do this with clauses connected by a coordinator:

> *For he was wearing a white suit I could easily spot him

Once we have shown our students that subordinators and coordinators exhibit
different syntactic characteristics in English it is easier to get them to accept and remember the differences between the two kinds of conjunctions in German.

German coordinators cannot function as clause elements (see §2.41), i.e. they
ake position zero in regard to word order. For example:

$$\underset{1}{\text{dann}} \; \underset{\text{FV-2}}{\text{sagte}} \; \text{ich} \ldots$$

$$\underset{0}{\text{und}} \; \underset{1}{\text{dann}} \; \underset{\text{FV-2}}{\text{sagte}} \; \text{ich} \ldots$$

German subordinators on the other hand can only introduce dependent clauses, i.e. clauses
in which the finite verb form occurs as the last element (see §2.82). For example:

$$\underset{\text{SUB}}{\text{weil}} \; \text{ich nicht mehr genau} \; \underset{\text{FV-L}}{\text{wusste}}, \ldots$$

$$\underset{\text{SUB}}{\text{als}} \; \text{ich endlich zum Bahnhof} \; \underset{\text{FV-L}}{\text{kam}} \; , \ldots$$

Some of our students find it very difficult to remember which of the German
conjunctions are coordinators and which are subordinators. In such cases we have found
it helpful to tell them to memorize the small number of the most common coordinators—
und, oder, denn, aber, sondern—and to proceed from there on the assumption that all other conjunctions are subordinators. We must not fail to point out the difference between
aber 'but (nevertheless)' and sondern 'but (on the contrary).' The latter occurs only after
negative statements.

4.62 PREPOSITIONS

As a part of speech, prepositions present no difficulties to the beginning student of German since they behave similarly in our two languages. Conflicts arise mostly
from the fact that German prepositions govern various cases. The prepositions can conveniently be divided into four groups (see §3.51):

preposition + accusative	(example: durch)
preposition + dative	(example: zu)
preposition + genitive	(example: während)
preposition + dative or accusative	(example: in)

It is evident that the fourth group causes special difficulties. We will discuss ways of
overcoming these difficulties and suggest relevant drills in §6.6.

| 4.7 | ADVERBS |

We end this brief discussion of the parts of speech in our two languages with a few remarks about <u>adverbs</u>. We mentioned above that this class called "adverb" (excluding those adverbs which are content words, see §4.5) is little more than a catchall, into which we put words which do not fit into any of the other classes.

4.71 GROUPS OF SPECIAL ADVERBS

Before we list and discuss those adverbs which are function words, we have to mention several groups of adverbs which differ formally from the bulk of adjective-adverbs which we have discussed above. You will remember that the form of those adverbs consisted simply of the stem of the corresponding or underlying adjective with a zero ending. For example:

SCHNELLe Wagen   vs.   Wagen fahren SCHNELL

The first group comprises adverbs derived from numerals; the corresponding adjectives —which can occur in attributive position only—are also listed:

| zweitens | drittens | viertens, etc. |
| zweit- | dritt- | viert- |

Then there is a closed class of adverbs denoting a position in space. From these adverbs we can form adjectives by the addition of the ending <u>-er</u>. It should be pointed out to the students that the resulting form is not a comparative, but the positive of an adjective which can only be used in attributive position. These adjectives are defective in that they do not inflect for a comparative, although they do inflect for the superlative. The following is the complete list:

adverb	attributive positive	attributive superlative
oben	ober-	oberst-
unten	unter-	unterst-
aussen	äusser-	äusserst-
innen	inner-	innerst-
mitten (in)	mittler-	mittelst-
vorne	vorder-	vorderst-
hinten	hinter-	hinterst-

A number of very frequent German adverbs form adjectives by adding the ending <u>-ig</u>. Again, these adjectives can only occur in attributive position. None of these adjectives inflect for comparison. They cause our students a great deal of trouble. Since English lacks comparable forms these German adjectives usually have to be translated by a prepositional phrase in English.

| hier | dort | diesseits | jenseits | auswärts | heute |
| hiesig- | dortig- | diesseitig- | jenseitig- | auswärtig- | heutig- |

| morgen | gestern | jetzt | damals | allein | sonst |
| morgig- | gestrig- | jetzig- | damalig- | alleinig- | sonstig- |

Ve conclude this section with a brief semantic survey of the most frequent adverbial func-
ion words of German:

	question form	"answer form"
cause	weshalb	deshalb
	warum	darum
time	wann	dann, immer, jetzt, nun, nie, noch, oft, wieder, eben, gerade, erst
place	wo	hier, dort, da
	wohin	hierhin, dorthin, dahin
	woher	hierher, daher
manner	wie	so
degree		fast, nur, kaum, sehr, zu, eher, etwas
		doch, denn, nicht, wohl, auch
stressed and final		ein, aus, auf, ab, hin, her, mit, etc.

COMPULSORY GRAMMATICAL CATEGORIES | 5

5.0 **INTRODUCTORY**

For many centuries grammarians have tried to discern a basic grammatical system that would be valid for all languages at all times. Although it now seems that most languages do have words which might be called substantives, and other words which might be called verbs, this search for a universal grammar has proved futile. Each language has evolved its own grammatical system and this system serves the needs of this particular language. Distinctions and types of expression that are necessary and fundamental in English, and which seem to us indispensable for proper communication, may not occur at all in Bavarian or Basque. Since English is our native language we are, of course, biased and tend to regard the distinctions which other languages have and English does not have as superfluous, at best needlessly pedantic. And yet, we can all agree that the universe surrounding us is an amorphous mass: all the things, the states, the happenings, and events in it are not neatly divided and classed, they are a continuum. Language, any language, on the other hand is discrete and selective: it dictates the ways in which we select and group elements of our experience. Thus it has often been said that the particular language we speak provides us with a kind of "grid" through which we perceive the world. The universe surrounding us is dissected along lines laid down by the various sub structures of our language. The GRAMMATICAL CATEGORIES which our language employs are one of these substructures, and, from what we have said, it is obvious that these grammatical categories differ from one language to another.

Why do we call these categories compulsory? Grammatical categories must be considered compulsory if proper communication in that language would become impossible in their absence. Perhaps this will become clearer if we cite an example involving an unnecessary grammatical category. Only a little more than 20 years ago the writer of these lines had to decline English nouns in class in the following manner:

the table	the tables
of the table	of the tables
to the table	to the tables
the table	the tables

We were taught that English nouns possessed a grammatical category case, and we were convinced that "the table" was an accusative singular whereas "to the tables" was a dative plural. It did not occur to us that we could—with equal justification—expand this paradigm to include an instrumental ("with the table") and a vocative ("oh table"). Certainly the only reason why this was not done lay in the fact that this particular grammar of English was written by a German who lacked the compulsory categories of vocative and instrumental, but who was equally sure about the universal necessity of a genitive, a dative, and an accusative.

"Language provides us with a grid through which we perceive the world." It follows that we have to recognize and acquire this new "grid" if we want to learn a second language. In this chapter we shall attempt to show the differences between the compulsory grammatical categories of English and German.

5.1 | SUBSTANTIVES

In order to keep our presentation clear, we will first deal with the compulsory grammatical categories as they apply to substantives, i.e. nouns, pronouns, adjectives, and determiners.

5.11 NUMBER

As we all know, NOUNS inflect for number in both English and German. Our students have therefore no trouble in grasping the fact that German nouns appear either in the singular or in the plural. The major difficulty lies not in the concept of plural but in the bewildering array of forms with which German nouns form the plural. Depending on their degree of linguistic sophistication, our students think that the plural marker of English nouns is always /-s/, or that it varies between /-s, -z, -iz/. Either concept tends to be transferred into German with the result that a form like Vaters is at first thought to be a plural. Since the plural forms of German nouns are almost completely unpredictable, it is best to tell the students that the plural form (as well as the gender, see below) is part of the intrinsic information which they have to know about a German noun before they can use it correctly. Thus we advise them to learn the equivalent of "father" not as Vater, but as der Vater, Väter.

Perhaps we should add a note here about certain English nouns which—though singular in form—take a verb in the plural and vice versa. As the examples show, no such nouns exist in German: a noun which is singular in form will always take a singular verb; a noun which is plural in form will always be followed by a verb in the plural form.

the United States is a large country

die Vereinigten Staaten sind ein grosses Land

the police have come

die Polizei ist gekommen

5.111 PRONOUNS

Pronouns also do not cause any difficulty in regard to their inflection for number. Both English and German personal pronouns inflect by suppletion, and thus it is mainly a question of learning the German forms. The German equivalents of <u>you</u> present special difficulties which we will discuss in §6.7.

5.112 DETERMINERS

The difficulties increase when we examine the behavior of the DETERMINER in our two languages. To be sure, English shows inflection for number in the case of <u>this</u> : <u>these</u> and <u>that</u> : <u>those</u>, but sometimes our students encounter a good deal of trouble in remembering that German shows inflection for number with <u>all</u> determiners.

5.113 ADJECTIVES

Since English ADJECTIVES are not inflected at all, the singular/plural (as well as case and gender) distinctions of German adjectives present without a doubt the greatest problem to the beginning student. As we have shown in the introduction to this chapter, the students tend to regard the inflectional endings of the German attributive adjectives as unnecessary. In general, however, our experience has been that the carry-over from noun inflection and the familiar idea of concord make it easy for them to accept the fact that German adjectives do inflect for number. Here again, though, the forms are bothersome and confusing. We need a great many drills to familiarize the student with the use of the adjective endings, and it takes a good deal of time before the correct choice becomes automatic.

5.12 CASE

The concept of CASE is, as we all know only too well, one of the hardest thing to teach to an American student. One of the main reasons for this is the impression that we have at least the remnants of a case system in Modern English. Of course this is true historically, but there is strong disagreement among grammarians about the number of cases in Modern English. Some writers name two (common case and genitive); some three (nominative, genitive, and objective); some four (nominative, genitive, dative, accusative) Some even name more than four (cf. P. Roberts, <u>Understanding Grammar</u>, p. 39). This di agreement is not a superficial dispute about terminology. It reflects a deep cleavage between two main schools of English grammatical thought—between those who put most emphasis on form and those who put most emphasis on function. We have seen this difference throughout our discussion of grammar, but nowhere does it manifest itself more strongly than in the treatment of case. We do not intend, of course, to enter into this discussion: we are solely interested in pointing out that as teachers of German we can never start out with a clean slate. Instead, our students invariably have had some grammatical instructio before they come to us, and thus we usually are faced with the problem of clearing up existing confusion and diverging opinions in their notions of English grammar before we can teach them any German grammar. Most grammarians, even the formalists, point out that English shows case distinctions in the genitive of nouns and in the objective (or accusative f several personal pronouns. But is this really so?

With reference to the teaching of German, there is no problem with a phrase like the boy's dog—but if we consider the so-called group genitive and contrast it with German usage we can easily see how baffling the problem of case is to our students. We speak of a group genitive in English if a phrase (often a prepositional phrase) rather than an unexpanded word is involved in a genitive construction. Modern English usage demands that the 's be put immediately before the noun modified by the genitive rather than immediately after the noun which is the center of the genitive expression, e.g. the President of the Board's daughter. Let us contrast such a construction with its German equivalent:

>Frederick the Great's policy
>Friedrichs des Grossen Politik

Since Modern English is apparently becoming more and more "elastic" in regard to the length of the phrase which appears in the "genitive case," it is easy to see that we cannot expect our students to grasp the essence of the German case system by pointing out to them that English has a genitive also. (Roberts cites this delightful though hardly elegant example: "the woman who was waiting for a bus on the corner in front of the Bank of America's purse . . .," p. 45.)

In regard to the pronouns there is no doubt that several have two clearly distinct forms: I : me, he : him, she : her, etc. But if we listen carefully to the type of English which our students speak—and this is after all the basis on which we must build—it soon becomes apparent that the choice of the pronoun form depends much less on syntactic function (case criteria) than on its position within the clause. In the position before the finite verb we usually get the nominative (common) form:

>I went home
>I was given a book

After the finite verb or after a preposition we find the oblique form:

>he gave me
>it is me
>for, with me

In pairs we usually get the nominative form:

>he and I
>between you and I

Compare these clauses:

>who was there?
>who did you see?
>with whom did you go?
>who did you go with?
>the man whom I know lives here
>the man whom I think lives here

Assuming the role of purists, we could, of course, tell our students that some of these uses are "incorrect," but we can't get away from the fact that this is the way th most of our young people speak and hence we have to conclude that for the vast majority of them the concept of <u>case</u> is completely new and alien.

To counter the notion that position has anything to do with case, we have to drill extensively with such patterns as:

$$\underset{\text{NOM}}{\underline{\text{der Junge}}} \text{ gab } \underset{\text{DAT}}{\underline{\text{der Frau}}} \underset{\text{ACC}}{\underline{\text{das Buch}}}$$

$$\underset{\text{NOM}}{\underline{\text{der Junge}}} \text{ gab } \underset{\text{ACC}}{\underline{\text{das Buch}}} \underset{\text{DAT}}{\underline{\text{der Frau}}}$$

$$\underset{\text{DAT}}{\underline{\text{der Frau}}} \text{ gab } \underset{\text{NOM}}{\underline{\text{der Junge}}} \underset{\text{ACC}}{\underline{\text{das Buch}}}$$

$$\underset{\text{ACC}}{\underline{\text{das Buch}}} \text{ gab } \underset{\text{NOM}}{\underline{\text{der Junge}}} \underset{\text{DAT}}{\underline{\text{der Frau}}}$$

(Other uses of case, e.g. with verbals and prepositions, have been dealt with briefly in §§ 3.221 and 3.51.)

5.13 GRAMMATICAL GENDER

Grammatical GENDER is another grammatical category which plays an impo tant, almost all-pervasive role in German and which is not matched by a comparable fea ture in English. The main source of the student's difficulties lies in the fact that English simply does not have gender in the <u>grammatical</u> sense of that term. Textbooks sometime make the situation even more complicated than it needs to be by saying that English has "natural gender." But this is really quite another matter and ought to be given a differen name. We do, of course, find between English nouns and pronouns the type of grammatic relationship which is called "cross reference." That is, we say "the boy—he," "the girl— she," "the table—it"; and we also say "the ship—she/it," "my jalopy—she/it," etc. But th is a vastly different thing from grammatical gender. The particular pronoun we use in cross reference is conditioned <u>not</u> by the grammatical class of the noun, but either by th meaning of the noun, by its referent (hence "the boy—he," "the girl—she"), or by our att tude toward it (hence "my jalopy—she"). As used in structures of modification, German gender is totally different. We all know that German says "die Frau" but "das Weib," "d Soldat" but "die Wache," or "der Wagen" but "das Auto," even though in each case the re erent, the meaning of the noun, is the same. In other words: gender in German has nothi to do with meaning, it is a grammatical classification of nouns. Every noun must be re ferred to by one, and always the same one regardless of attitude, of the three pronouns e <u>sie</u>, <u>es</u>. In a few instances the gender serves as the sole distinction between otherwise id tical nouns, e.g. <u>der See</u> 'lake' vs. <u>die See</u> 'sea.'

It is very unfortunate, indeed, that we do not have a different set of names to refer to the three grammatical genders of German. Our terms masculine, feminine, and neuter almost invariably persuade the student that gender, even grammatical gender, is somehow linked with sex—an ever present association for students anywhere. We have e perimented with using terms like <u>der</u>-word etc., but this has proved useless, since there is always one student who will ask, "Is that the same as masculine in French (in Latin,

.)?" The terms masculine, feminine, and neuter are so well established—they have en used for centuries—that we cannot now abandon them. We must do all we can to per- ade our students that they are nothing more than mere grammatical labels. We must not ow them to go through life believing that the Germans somehow consider spoons (der ffel) to be masculine, forks (die Gabel) to be feminine, and knives (das Messer) to be ither. German simply has a three-way distinction in regard to the modifiers which a ven noun can take, and this distinction is called gender.

It follows that the gender of a German noun is not predictable; it simply will ve to be learned along with the meaning of every new noun that comes up in the course. very good grammar has a list of those noun suffixes which allow us to predict the gen- r of a limited number of nouns.) It is also perfectly understandable that our students ve to overcome an emotional barrier in learning the gender of nouns, since to them it a completely superfluous feature, and to a speaker of English there seems to be no log- al reason why he should burden himself with this unnecessary information. We must be ick to point out that the student simply cannot use a noun unless he knows its gender, nce the choice of every modifier or relative will depend on this knowledge.

In a few rare instances so-called natural gender does appear in German. ords like Schildwache or Mädchen must be referred to as sie and es respectively, if the ference is a close one; but they can be, and usually are, referred to as er and sie if the ference is further away. For example:

> das Mädchen, das ich gestern kennengelernt habe, geht auch in die
> Albrechtschule. Wir tranken eine Tasse Kaffee miteinander und sie
> erzählte mir, . . .

5.2 VERBS

In the chapters on Phrase Structure and Parts of Speech we have had occasion mention briefly some of the grammatical categories of VERBS. Here we will take a oser look at those features which are likely to prove difficult to our students.

5.21 PERSON-NUMBER

The first difficulty which we usually encounter when introducing German verbs the PERSON-NUMBER category. Perhaps we can best show the major areas of conflict we contrast the English with the German system by the number of differing forms in the resent tense.

3	2	1
is	works	
am	work	can
are		

English has a maximum of three distinctions, but only for one verb, be, which acts irregularly in almost all other respects as well. Most verbs show two distinct forms, and a
handful show only one form. Let us now take a look at the strikingly different arrangements in German:

5	5	4	4	4	3
sind	sprechen	kommen	lesen	können	sitzen
bin	spreche	komme	lese	kann	sitze
ist	spricht	kommt	liest		sitzt
seid	sprecht		lest	könnt	
bist	sprichst	kommst	liest	kannst	

We have found that it is generally not too difficult to get students to accept the idea of
multiple person-number distinctions since the concept as such is not new to them, c.f.
On the other hand, students find it very hard to learn and to remember the forms which
they know they should use. Only a good deal of time spent on relevant drills will produce
results.

5.22 INFINITIVE

In general, the INFINITIVE causes no problem since verbs in both languages
have this form. In either language there is only one verb which has a special form for the
infinitive: be and sein. In all other cases the infinitive is identical in form with the first
person plural present indicative.

A number of English verbs, the so-called modal auxiliaries (cf. §3.13), do not
have an infinitive form. Instead we have to use some periphrastic construction or other
substitute (suppletion). This creates a problem only in so far as our beginning students
tend to use these suppletions (or rather their literal equivalents) in German as well. We
have to be aware of this difficulty and design drills involving the infinitive forms of the
modal auxiliaries.

5.23 PAST PARTICIPLE

The PAST PARTICIPLE does not usually pose problems, although once again
students find it hard to master the forms. Both English and German use participles as adjectives also, and when so used they present the same difficulties as descriptive adjectives
(c.f. §§4.51 and 5.113). In verbal phrases involving a past participle the choice of an auxiliary creates a problem. We have dealt with this question in §§3.122 and 6.34.

5.24 PRESENT PARTICIPLE

The PRESENT PARTICIPLE is likely to be troublesome since its literal English equivalent, the -ing form, is used in several fundamentally different functions, and
students have a great deal of difficulty keeping these functions apart. There is no one Ger

an construction which will correspond to all the functions of English -ing. Hence we will
ve to describe the various functions of the -ing form separately and list their different
rman counterparts.

5.241 -ING FORMS AS ADJECTIVES

If the present participle functions as an adjective formed from a verb, the
ansfer into German is easy:

a biting dog	ein beissender Hund
a charming girl	ein reizendes Mädchen

But English uses the present participle also in combinations with another
rb. For example:

he was sitting in the bathtub <u>singing</u>
he spent a month by the sea <u>recuperating</u>

 such sentences German does not use the present participle. Instead, we generally find
construction involving two finite verb forms:

er sass in der Badewanne <u>und sang</u>
er verbrachte einen Monat am Meer <u>und erholte sich</u>

ie verb <u>kommen</u> presents an exception to this since German uses the <u>past</u> participle of
e second verb with it:

he came <u>bicycling</u> into the village
er kam ins Dorf <u>geradelt</u>

5.242 -ING FORMS AS NOUNS

The <u>-ing</u> form is frequently used as a verbal noun, i.e. a noun expressing the
tion of the underlying verb. This use is sometimes called the <u>gerund</u>. Its most frequent
unterpart in German is a neuter noun made from the infinitive of the verb.

who taught you <u>bowling</u>?   wer hat Ihnen <u>das Kegeln</u> beigebracht?

ry often German may substitute nouns which are not identical in form with the infini-
e. For example:

the proper <u>feeding</u> of lions	<u>das</u> richtige <u>Füttern</u> von Löwen
	<u>die</u> richtige <u>Fütterung</u> von Löwen

te how easily the use of the gerund overlaps with that of the present participle in Eng-
h:

by properly <u>feeding</u> the lions	durch <u>das</u> richtige <u>Füttern</u> der Löwen
	durch <u>die</u> richtige <u>Fütterung</u> der Löwen

st commonly we can translate the English construction <u>by</u> + -ing by a German clause
durch dass SUBJECT + FINITE VERB, although this German construction is often con-
lered somewhat clumsy. For example:

by paying now you can save

man kann sparen dadurch, dass man jetzt zahlt

Note also the German equivalents of the parallel English constructions:

while + -ing

when + -ing

while sitting in the bathtub he sang

während er in der Badewanne sass, sang er

when sitting in the bathtub he sings

wenn er in der Badewanne sitzt, singt er

Special attention must be paid to the frequent English constructions involving instead of -ing and without -ing which are rendered in German by marked infinitives, somewhat on a par with the English construction in order to. For example:

he ran instead of walking

er lief anstatt zu gehen

he drove by without stopping

er fuhr vorbei ohne zu halten

he left (in order) to buy stamps

er ging weg, um Briefmarken zu kaufen

5.243 -ING FORMS AS VERBALS

We have deliberately postponed mentioning the most common use of -ing: the so-called progressive form. As we have pointed out elsewhere (§3.1222), German has no equivalent to such verb phrases and invariably uses a finite verb form instead. For example:

he is going to the movies

er geht ins Kino

5.25 REFLEXIVE

In both German and English we find a special class of verbs which is usually called REFLEXIVE, i.e. the verb is followed by a reflexive pronoun. Such a pronoun shows the action of the verb returning to the subject instead of passing to some other object. Hence, in a reflexive construction the subject and the object of the verb are the same. This construction is common with a great many English verbs: "I hurt myself," "we enjoyed ourselves," "he killed himself." Very often we can choose in English whether to express the reflexive or not:

he shaved = he shaved himself

Sometimes the reflexive is used after a preposition, but commonly the simple pronoun is preferred in this syntactic environment:

throw the blanket over yourself = throw the blanket over you

ese compound personal pronouns (i.e. personal pronoun + -self) may also be used as
ensifiers without change of form. The following example will illustrate this use:

she washed the shirt herself

ry often the intensifying pronouns appear immediately after the governing substantive:

she herself washed the shirt

te that this flexibility of word order is present only when the compound pronouns are
ed as intensifiers, but not when they are used as reflexives. Contrast these two clauses:

she washed (herself)
she herself washed   (all the laundry)

is true that the second example is not likely to occur without an explicit object. It is
so true that even without the object ("all the laundry") these two clauses are distin-
ished not just by word order but also by a different stress distribution. Nevertheless,
compound pronouns are used in two vastly different functions, and—at least on paper
hey are identical in form.

If we examine the corresponding situation in German, one area of conflict be-
mes apparent immediately. German cannot use its reflexive pronouns as intensifiers;
stead it uses a particle which is uninflected: selbst or selber. Since the two uses of the
glish compound pronoun are expressed in a totally different manner in German, it is
vious that we must make sure that our students can distinguish reflexive from intensi-
ng use in English. In the actual classroom situation word order and stress, as pointed
t above, have proved more reliable and effective criteria than meaning. Once the differ-
ce is clearly established, students react with relief to the immutability of selbst.

We have seen that English often leaves us a choice as to whether or not we
nt to state the reflexive pronoun explicitly. This is not true in German: if a reflexive
uation is to be described, the reflexive pronoun has to be used. Note the contrast be-
een these two sentences:

ich habe mich gewaschen   I washed (myself)
ich habe gewaschen   I did the laundry

is holds true after prepositions as well, and in this situation it very often causes the
dents to make mistakes. For example:

er zog die Decke über sich   he pulled the blanket over him(self)
er zog die Decke über ihn   he pulled the blanket over him (=some-
                                       body else)

                                       er hat sich bekleckert
he got jam all over him
                                       er hat ihn bekleckert

In general we can say that the reflexive pronoun is used much more frequent-
in German than in English. Compare these examples:

the book reads well	das Buch liest <u>sich</u> gut
the suit wears well	der Anzug trägt <u>sich</u> gut

Very often German introduces an additional verbal element (<u>lassen</u>, see also §6.35) in d⟨ scribing reflexive situations:

the book sells well	das Buch <u>lässt sich</u> gut verkaufen
this paper cuts easily	das Papier <u>lässt sich</u> gut schneiden

Finally, we have to mention a fairly large group of German verbs which never appear w⟨ out a direct object, i.e. which must appear with the reflexive pronoun unless some othe⟨ explicit object is present. Such verbs exist in English also, but their number is negligib⟨ For example:

we enjoyed the party
we enjoyed ourselves
*we enjoyed

Note the different behavior of <u>wechseln</u> and <u>ändern</u> 'change':

he changed the colors
    er wechselte die Farben   =   er änderte die Farben

the colors changed
    die Farben wechselten   ≠   die Farben änderten <u>sich</u>

Verbs which behave like <u>ändern</u> are more numerous than is commonly assumed, and since most of our dictionaries and textbooks fail to mention this peculiarity the number of mistakes is proportionately high. The <u>Minimum Standard German Vocabu</u> lary (Wadepuhl and Morgan, 1939) contains the following: <u>bewegen</u>, <u>biegen</u>, <u>bilden</u>, <u>dehne</u>⟨ <u>drehen</u>, <u>entzünden</u>, <u>füllen</u>, <u>heben</u>, <u>lösen</u>, <u>öffnen</u>, <u>schliessen</u>, <u>mischen</u>, <u>aufladen</u> 'to charge⟨ <u>strecken</u>, <u>tragen</u>, <u>erholen</u>.

COMPULSORY 6
SEMANTIC
CATEGORIES

6.0 | INTRODUCTORY

In the preceding chapter we talked about the ways in which the grammatical
categories of our native language color our thinking and how they interfere with the learning of a second language. We spoke of a kind of filter, a "grid" formed by the grammatical
categories through which we perceive the universe. The workings of such a grid—of which
we are usually unaware until we go beyond the confines of our native speech—become even
more apparent if we leave the field of grammar and enter that of semantics. Now, the
more we know about two languages the more obvious it becomes that a full description of
the semantics of two languages would be limitless in the full sense of this word: if we
were to describe the lexical contrasts of English and German we would have to give first
full descriptions of the universe as seen by a speaker of English, then of the universe as
seen by a speaker of German, and finally we would have to point out where these concep-
tions of the world differ. With a little reflection it becomes apparent that such complete
descriptions—even if they were possible and feasible—would be so lengthy and cumbersome as to be unusable. For example: all of us that have been to Germany know that a
Wald looks and feels different from a <u>forest</u>. Granted that it were possible to differentiate
clearly the physical characteristics, how are we to describe the ways in which Americans
feel and think about the <u>forest</u> as against the ways in which Germans feel and think about
their <u>Wald</u>? Obviously such an undertaking would be doomed to failure. But even if it were
successful, how could we in the classroom use such a description to advantage?

We all know that as we go from English into German we notice that almost every single lexical item, every word, differs in some way or other in its syntactic range,
in its morphological range, its denotative range, its connotative range, or in its circumstantial range. Let us examine a few examples to see what is meant by these various terms.

Both <u>sleep</u> and <u>schlafen</u> occur as transitive verbs, but they differ in their <u>syn-
tactic range</u>. In English we can say things like:

this cabin sleeps two

German usage is restricted to such sentences as (cognate object sentences):

er schläft den Schlaf der Gerechten

Words in our two languages differ in their morphological range; and through false analo
our students make a good many mistakes. We have picked the suffix -lich at random:

Mann	männlich	man	manly
Tag	täglich	day	daily
Haus	häuslich	house	-
Heim	(heimlich)	home	(homely)
	heimelig		homey
	heimisch		(at home)

Our students learn early that find corresponds to German finden, and this lexical equati
will do very well for a time. And yet the denotative range of finden is much narrower th
that of find, since finden is always limited to the denotation 'to find by chance even thou
a considerable effort may be involved.' Compare:

let me find you a chair
*ich werde Ihnen einen Stuhl finden
ich werde Ihnen einen Stuhl suchen, besorgen, etc.

Differences in the connotative range are even harder to describe. The range of connota-
tions carried by Freund, Freundschaft is much wider than that of friend, friendship; sta
differently: it is much easier to find a friend than a Freund. A sentence such as "In den
ersten zwei Wochen habe ich viele Freundschaften geschlossen" strikes a German as st
ing an impossibility, if not a downright lie, whereas the literal English equivalent is pe
fectly acceptable and understandable:

I made many friends in the first two weeks.

If we are aware of the differences in connotative range between friends and Freunde, w
will have to translate the English sentence as:

In den ersten zwei Wochen habe ich viele Bekanntschaften gemacht.

Finally, we should like to give an example of differences in the circumstantial range of
words in our two languages. Very early in the course the student learns that danke mea
thank you. And yet, when these words are uttered in reply to an offer of some sort, thei
meanings contrast sharply. For example:

would you like a cigarette?   thank you (yes, I'll take one)
darf ich Ihnen eine Zigarette anbieten?   danke (nein, jetzt nicht)

This lexical contrast may (and does) lead to embarrassing situations which we can avoi
by pointing out the differences in circumstantial range between the words and expressic
of English and German.

By citing these few examples, we wished to point out that the ranges of lexi
items ("words") exist only in a given language and are uniquely integrated in much the
same way as the phonetic ranges of a phoneme have no existence outside a given phonol

al system. We cannot expect, therefore, that the various ranges of a German lexical
m (its "Wortfeld") will correspond to those of an English lexical item. Yet our students
e led to believe by the vocabulary lists of many of our textbooks that such one-to-one
xical correspondences exist, or at least that they are the rule. It is obvious that in or-
r to give the student full control of a newly learned word we have to put him in com-
and of the various ranges which this word possesses. We know that this can only be done
adually, but the eventual full grasp of all the meanings of a given word is necessary if
 are to counteract the tendencies shown by the student as he learns German: the projec-
n of the patterns of English upon the units of German, his failure to assimilate patterns
t parallel to those of his own system, and the building-up of false analogies based on
tterns which he did observe in German. It goes without saying that only a competent
acher who himself is aware of the differences in the ranges of English and German
rds can convey these differences to the students and can control the growth of the stu-
nt's vocabulary in such a way as to avoid the formation of false analogies.

6.1 COMPULSORY SEMANTIC CATEGORIES

We have shown that a discussion of the various semantic ranges of individual
xical items would go beyond the limits of this study. However, quite apart from the se-
antics of individual words or groups of words there exist in our two languages different
ts of compulsory semantic categories, and a description of the structure of these se-
antic categories and how they differ will prove helpful to our students. Sometimes it is
ficult to draw the line between grammatical and semantic categories, particularly in an
vestigation of this sort which deals with two languages concurrently. If we were to de-
ribe only German, there is little doubt that the subjunctive, for example, should be dealt
th under the heading of grammatical categories. But since English does not have a for-
al grammatical category which we might call subjunctive, it follows that we first have
 establish such a category in our students' minds. We have found that most of the diffi-
lties which our English-speaking students encounter are of a semantic nature, i.e. they
ve more trouble determining when and why to use a subjunctive than how to use it.

6.11 SUBJUNCTIVE

Thus we will discuss the SUBJUNCTIVE as our first semantic category. We
ve a few remarks about it when we discussed auxiliaries (see §3.1213), but it might be
ll to repeat some of our introductory statements here. In English we find that the use
 the subjunctive is extremely rare. Nevertheless, it should be useful to show our stu-
nts that the difference in meaning between

    I insist that he <u>lives</u> here   [and]
    I insist that he <u>live</u> here

mes solely from the opposition of indicative vs. subjunctive. Thus we can point out that
most all English verbs inflect for a subjunctive mood, though only in this one form, and

only by zero inflection. It is true, of course, that there is not a single verb form in English which could be unambiguously labeled a subjunctive. That is to say, though a form may be a subjunctive (e.g. <u>live</u> in the example cited), it always happens to look like some indicative form. Thus, a formal definition of the English subjunctive proves to be very difficult. A notional definition of the subjunctive mood in English is even more inconclusive; the matter of mood becomes pure philosophic speculation and as such has little relation to grammar. In its simplest form the student's problem can be stated thus:

$$
\text{(he) had}
\begin{cases}
\text{(er) hatte} \\
\text{(er) hätte} \\
\text{(er) habe}
\end{cases}
$$

That is to say: in theory the student is confronted with a choice of three German forms whenever he is about to put an English verb in the Past modification into German. Since we have been unable to find a conclusive grammatical axiom which might determine the correct choice, we are forced to create a new compulsory semantic category in the student's way of thinking. Fortunately, the problem appears not as formidable in practice. For one thing, indicative forms are much more frequent than subjunctive forms. Second, English does show distinctions semantically comparable to the German category of subjunctive, if we are willing to go beyond the confines of verb inflection and look at syntactic rather than morphological entities.

6.111 UNREAL CONDITIONS

We have found it most useful to begin our presentation of the German subjunctive with a comparison of an English "when-clause" with an "if-clause":

when I <u>had</u> enough money	I went to Europe
if I <u>had</u> enough money	I would go to Europe
	I could go to Europe
	I might go to Europe
	(I should go to Europe)

In contrastive frames such as this, our students readily see the semantic difference in the function of the formally identical <u>had's</u>. We point out to them that <u>had</u> in the "if-clause" is void of any time-signaling content and is compatible with any contextual clues specifying future or present chronology:

> if I <u>had</u> enough money <u>right now</u> . . .
> if I <u>had</u> enough money by <u>tomorrow</u> . . .

In this way we can prove to our students that "if + Past modification" signals not past chronology but uncertainty, unreality, improbability if an associated construction contains <u>would</u>/<u>could</u>/<u>might</u>/<u>should</u>. Once our students have accepted the fact that the two identical verb forms differ radically in function we can tell them that many German verbs express this difference in <u>function</u> in their <u>forms</u> as well.

als ich genug Geld <u>hatte</u>, fuhr ich nach Europa

wenn ich genug Geld <u>hätte</u>, würde ich nach Europa fahren

Sometimes our students fail to grasp the fact that the Past modification of the English verb is an essential part of this construction. They erroneously conclude that all "f-clauses" demand subjunctive forms in German. We counter this notion by contrasting:

<u>if</u> I <u>have</u> enough money I will go to Europe

<u>if</u> I <u>had</u> enough money I would go to Europe

<u>wenn</u> ich genug Geld <u>habe</u>, fahre ich nach Europa

<u>wenn</u> ich genug Geld <u>hätte</u>, würde ich nach Europa fahren

t this point in the presentation of the new semantic category of subjunctive we have found helpful to pause and to drill extensively on the pattern of these formulas:

<u>if</u> . . . . Past + <u>would</u>/<u>could</u>/<u>might</u>/<u>should</u> . . . infinitive
<u>wenn</u> . . . general subjunctive + <u>würde</u>, etc. . . . . infinitive

Only when this primary pattern is securely established can we go on by demonstrating the freedom of arrangement which exists in Modern German. Since no such eedom exists in English, many of our students experience considerable confusion in this aspect.

1) wenn sie flöge, würde sie schneller hinüberkommen
2) wenn sie flöge, käme sie schneller hinüber
3) wenn sie fliegen würde, käme sie schneller hinüber
4) wenn sie fliegen würde, würde sie schneller hinüberkommen

Some grammarians still insist that only (1) is correct, but we find that the other three possibilities are becoming more and more common. Many Germans feel, however, at (4) is rather clumsy; we should therefore avoid it in the classroom. The "würde-rases" occur most frequently with regular weak verbs since such verbs do not have a istinctive form for the general subjunctive.

6.112 CONTRARY-TO-FACT STATEMENTS IN PAST TENSE

"If" + <u>had</u> + participle and <u>would</u>/<u>could</u>/<u>might</u>/<u>should</u> + <u>have</u> + participle in an associated construction signals the meaning contrary-to-fact in past time. For example:

if I <u>had known</u> that you were coming I <u>would have baked</u> a cake

his sentence obviously means that no cake was baked since I did not know that you were oming. This meaning contrary-to-fact in the past is again expressed by the general subjunctive in German and we should point out the one-to-one correspondence of the various erb forms:

if I <u>had known</u> . . .

wenn ich <u>gewusst hätte</u>, (dass) . . .

I <u>would have baked</u> . . .

<u>würde</u> ich . . . <u>gebacken haben</u>

More common than the verbal phrases <u>würde</u> + participle + <u>haben</u> and <u>würde</u> + participle + <u>sein</u> are the shorter phrases:

<u>hätte</u> + participle

<u>wäre</u> + participle

It has been our experience that students have little difficulty with the past contrary-to-fact application of the subjunctive provided that they have first become quite familiar with the use of the subjunctive in statements implying improbability, uncertainty, and unreality (§6.111).

6.113 OMISSION OF *WENN;* USE OF *SO, DANN*

In conditional clauses of the contrary-to-fact type, English structure allows us to omit "if" and to signal its meaning by the inversion of the sequence of subject and verb:

if I had known   =   had I known

Most of our students seem to feel that such inverted clauses are old-fashioned and they tend to avoid them at least in speaking. Therefore, we have to emphasize the fact that the omission of <u>wenn</u> and the occurrence of the finite verb form in its place is a feature of German which is (a) very much alive and often used in speaking as well as in writing, and (b) not restricted to contrary-to-fact clauses but occurring in all types of conditional clauses which may be introduced by <u>wenn</u>, i.e. real conditions, unreal conditions, and contrary-to-fact clauses. For example:

hat man gerade eine Operation durchgemacht,

<u>dann/so</u> braucht man ein bisschen Erholung

wäre ich an seiner Stelle,

<u>dann/so</u> würde ich's ganz anders anpacken

wären wir nicht so lange geblieben,

<u>dann/so</u> hätten wir den Zug jetzt nicht verpasst

Notice that the "follow-up clause" in the above sentences is introduced by either <u>dann</u> or <u>so</u>. This use of <u>dann/so</u> is very common after the conditional inversion, but it is not necessary. For example:

ginge er schneller, würde er rechtzeitig ankommen

ginge er schneller, <u>dann</u> würde er rechtzeitig ankommen

ginge er schneller, <u>so</u> würde er rechtzeitig ankommen

The occurrence of <u>dann/so</u> is not restricted to sentences which are introduced by a clause in which <u>wenn</u> is omitted. In colloquial German <u>dann/so</u> occur very frequently in conditional sentences which contain two <u>würde</u> + infinitive phrases. We have stated above (§6.111) that such sentences are considered inelegant and clumsy by the Germans. They occur nevertheless, particularly if two weak verbs are involved, since these do not ow distinctive forms in the general subjunctive. To avoid two successive <u>würde's</u>, <u>dann/</u> are inserted. For example:

wenn er fleissiger arbeiten würde, würde er mehr verdienen
wenn er fleissiger arbeiten würde, <u>dann</u> würde er mehr verdienen
wenn er fleissiger arbeiten würde, <u>so</u> würde er mehr verdienen

te that these two words merely function as markers: they signal the beginning of the ollow-up clause." In translating into English, our students have no trouble with <u>dann</u>: e literal equivalent 'then' usually fits into the English clause, although it is quite unnec- sary:

if he walked faster (<u>then</u>) he'd arrive on time

he other marker, <u>so</u>, causes a great deal of confusion since its literal equivalent 'so' akes no sense when used to introduce the "follow-up clause." We must make it a special int to tell our students that this <u>so</u> is not to be translated at all, that it is only a signal mark the beginning of the clause.

When they introduce "follow-up clauses," <u>so</u> and <u>dann</u> do not function as clause ements, i.e. they do not affect word order (cf. §2.41). Compare these sentences:

<u>ginge er schneller</u>, <u>würde</u> er rechtzeitig <u>ankommen</u>
     1   FV-2   INF

<u>ginge er schneller</u>, <u>dann würde</u> er rechtzeitig <u>ankommen</u>
     1   0 FV-2   INF

<u>ginge er schneller</u>, <u>so würde</u> er rechtzeitig <u>ankommen</u>
     1   0 FV-2   INF

Remember, however, that <u>dann</u> and <u>so</u> do function as clause elements in all ther uses. For example:

er liess nicht nach <u>und so gab</u> ich ihm schliesslich meine Zustimmung
                     CC 1 FV-2

sie küsste ihn <u>und dann fing</u> sie plötzlich zu weinen an
              CC 1 FV-2

6.114 OMISSION OF *WENN*-CLAUSE

So far we have discussed the use of the subjunctive in conditional clauses on- y. If matters rested here our task would be simple, but we must remember that this new ompulsory semantic category which we have to establish in our students' minds covers large number of linguistic situations whose only connection is that they suggest some- hing which is imaginable though not necessarily true—something which appeals to the earer's imagination without direct relevance to the facts or to his knowledge of such acts. Thus the subjunctive usually describes an action which is only imaginary, which asn't happened yet or which can't happen in the speaker's opinion.

Many clauses with the finite verb in the subjunctive are close to being frag- ments, i.e. they may be thought of as unreal conditions in which the "if-clause" has been eft out. German uses the subjunctive in sentences corresponding to the English type: "you could have been more considerate." For example:

> jetzt könnte er schon Arzt sein
> > (wenn er damals weiterstudiert hätte)
>
> ich würde ins Kino gehen
> > (wenn mir Vater Geld geschickt hätte)

Often the meaning of the wenn-clause is expressed by other means:

> mit besseren Empfehlungen könnten Sie in meiner Abteilung unterkommen
> > (but you don't have good recommendations and so I can't hire you)
>
> bei schönem Wetter gingen wir jetzt spazieren
> > (but it's raining and so we can't)

But then there are a considerable number of subjunctive clauses where nothing is "implied" or "left out," e.g.

> ich möchte sofort nach Europa fliegen
> ich könnte das nicht tun

6.115 OTHER USES OF THE SUBJUNCTIVE

Perhaps the best way to describe the various applications of the subjunctive is to group them according to the connotative meanings which they express. Aside from unreal conditions, the subjunctive is most often used as a means of indicating politeness. This use of the subjunctive is more frequent in the southern parts of the German-speaking area, particularly in Austria and Bavaria. In discussing it in class, it has proved helpful to remind our students of similar variations in English. For example:

I want some cigarettes	: I'd like some cigarettes
Can I have the car tonight?	: Could I have the car tonight?
Is it too much trouble?	: Would it be too much trouble?
können Sie mir sagen . . .	: könnten Sie mir sagen . . .
ist das nicht zuviel verlangt?	: wäre das nicht zuviel verlangt?
bringen Sie mir bitte das Buch mit	: brächten Sie mir bitte das Buch mit
was empfehlen Sie?	: was würden Sie empfehlen?
ein Taxi ist bequemer	: ein Taxi wäre bequemer

In Vienna or Munich this use of the subjective is sometimes carried to such extremes that other German speakers are greatly amused. For example:

> das Deutsche Museum wäre bei der Ludwigsbrücke
> Sie könnten vielleicht hier über die Strasse gehen
> das Bier wäre dort sehr gut
> womit könnte ich Ihnen dienen
> was dürfte ich Ihnen bringen

Next in decreasing order of frequency is the use of the subjunctive in unreal or hypothetical comparisons. Such comparisons are introduced by als ob, als wenn, or simply als ith inversion, cf. §6.113). For example:

tun Sie so, als wenn Sie zu Hause wären
tun Sie so, als ob Sie zu Hause wären
tun Sie so, als wären Sie zu Hause

the hypothetical comparison depends on an adjective, then als dass serves as the clause
troducer. For example:

es ist schon zu spät, als dass mein Mann noch im Büro wäre
ich habe zu wenig Geld, als dass ich mir einen Mercedes leisten könnte

ite frequently we find the subjunctive used to express unreal or unfulfillable wishes.
is is comparable to English use in certain idioms of the type "if I were you," "wish you
re here." In most cases the words nur or doch occur in such clauses. For example:

hätte ich doch diesen Fehler nicht gemacht
hätte ich das nur gewusst
wenn nur mein Vater käme
wenn mein Vater doch käme
käme mein Vater doch

an event at the very last moment fails to occur, German frequently describes what al-
ost happened by using the subjunctive together with fast or beinahe:

er wäre fast aus dem Fenster gefallen
sie hätte beinahe die Prüfung nicht bestanden

ne subjunctive is also used in questions which convey a strong element of doubt:

hätte er mir tatsächlich nur helfen wollen?
sollte er schon wieder verschlafen haben?
gäben Sie mir wirklich die Erlaubnis?

urthermore, the subjunctive is used in dependent clauses introduced by ohne dass if we
ish to describe an event which did not happen although we had every reason to assume
at it would or should. For example:

sie nahm einfach meinen Wagen,
                ohne dass sie mich darum gebeten hätte

er verliess das Konferenzzimmer,
                ohne dass er sich dazu geäussert hätte

e should point out that such ohne dass-clauses tend to be used less and less. Instead,
ermans now prefer the ohne zu constructions (cf. §5.242):

er verliess das Konferenzzimmer,
                ohne sich dazu geäussert zu haben

6.12 GENERAL AND SPECIAL SUBJUNCTIVE

Up to now we have postponed mentioning that there are two kinds of subjunctives in German, variously called general subjunctive vs. special subjunctive, past subjunctive vs. present subjunctive, unreal form vs. quotative form. For reasons given in §2.3, we have chosen the terms general vs. special subjunctive. So far we have dealt only with the general subjunctive: its use is far more common than that of the special subjunctive, and it should therefore be covered first in the teaching of German. The occurrence of the special subjunctive is now almost completely restricted to the written language. In speaking, Germans replace it either by the general subjunctive or by the corresponding indicative forms. This is not true, of course, for certain fixed formulas, such as

lang lebe der König	long live the king
Gott sei Dank	thank God [goodness]
Gott segne dich	God bless you (but never in the sense of Gesundheit!)

Aside from these idiomatic formulas, the special subjunctive is almost exclusively used to indicate that a statement is quoted indirectly. This application of the special subjunctive is found most frequently in expository prose—often also in scholarly publications. When an English writer paraphrases ideas quoted from someone else, he must keep on reminding the reader that he is quoting. This is usually done by the insertion of short phrases of the type: "(he) goes on to say, states furthermore, continues, adds," etc. In German these little reminders are superfluous: once the author has stated the origin of his quote, he will simply continue using the verb forms of the special subjunctive (or the general subjunctive) for the duration of the quote. The reader will thus know at all times that he is not reading the author's own opinion but somebody else's. For example:

> Paul Roberts schreibt, dass es wenig Sinn habe, im Englischen über verschiedene Modalformen zu sprechen. Eine inhaltbezogene Definition des Konjunktivs sei nahezu unmöglich. Auch die Beschreibung formaler Kriterien stosse auf grosse Schwierigkeiten, doch lasse sich hier ein Unterschied erkennen, zumindest in der 3. Person Singular. Was den Konjunktiv der Vergangenheit betreffe, so scheine es ihm am besten, diesen Begriff auf das Verbum 'to be' zu beschränken, weil es das einzige sei, das einen Unterschied in der Form beibehalten habe.

We should emphasize, however, that the forms of the general subjunctive have become much more popular even in passages such as the one cited as an example. A good many German writers seem to feel that the special subjunctive forms are obsolescent and they use these forms less and less. Thus, our example would be far more likely to appear in this form in a German article:

> Roberts schreibt, dass es wenig Sinn hätte, im Englischen über verschiedene Modalformen zu sprechen. Eine inhaltbezogene Definition des Konjunktivs wäre nahezu unmöglich. Auch die Beschreibung formaler Kriterien stiesse auf grosse Schwierigkeiten, etc.

It should be noted that the rival forms habe : hätte, sei : wäre, stosse : stiesse, etc. are completely devoid of any time-signaling content: they do not have any relevance to chrono

ical time. Similarly, the use of the subjunctive in German is not subject to any rules in
ard to sequence of tenses. Often it has proved very difficult to get this latter point
oss to our students. In translation exercises we have to design special drills to direct
student's attention to the fact that it is the <u>introductory verb</u> (in our example: <u>schreibt</u>)
t determines the tense of the English verbs which translate the German subjunctive
ms. For example:

> 1) Roberts schreibt, dass es wenig Sinn <u>habe</u>, . . .
>   Roberts schreibt, dass es wenig Sinn <u>hätte</u>, . . .
>   Roberts writes that there <u>is</u> little sense in . . .
>
> 2) Roberts schrieb, dass es wenig Sinn <u>habe</u>, . . .
>   Roberts schrieb, dass es wenig Sinn <u>hätte</u>, . . .
>   Roberts wrote that there <u>was</u> little sense in . . .

mming up: If the introductory verb is in the present, either subjunctive is usually trans-
ted by an English present. If the introductory verb is in a past form, either subjunctive
rm is usually translated by an English past form.

6.121 IMPERATIVE USE OF SPECIAL SUBJUNCTIVE

The forms of the special subjunctive are also used as a kind of 1st and 3d per-
n imperative. We have briefly mentioned this feature of the special subjunctive in our
scussion of clause types (cf. §2.51). If the verbal does not occur in the 3d person singu-
r, such clauses are often not clearly marked, since only the verb <u>sein</u> has special sub-
unctive forms which are clearly distinguished in all persons from the indicative forms.
he most common use of this form is in the "let us" type of request:

> sprechen wir nicht mehr davon!
> gehen wir (doch) ins Kino!

is also used in instructions to the reader, in recipes, prescriptions, etc. Note that the
erb may occur either in position 1 or 2 (cf. §2.51):

> man <u>denke</u> dabei nur an Laos . . .
> <u>gebe</u> Gott, dass . . .
> erst <u>gebe</u> man einen Löffel Neskaffee in die Tasse
> dann <u>giesse</u> man heisses Wasser nach
> und <u>rühre</u> fest um
> man <u>nehme</u> täglich 3 Tropfen auf nüchternen Magen

6.122 *DAMIT*-CLAUSES

Closely related to the application which we described in the preceding paragraph is the use of the special subjunctive in clauses introduced by <u>damit</u> (rarely, and
frowned upon by grammarians: <u>sodass</u>). For example:

> ich habe ihm eigenes Geld gegeben, <u>damit</u> er nach München <u>fahre</u>
> sie brachte ihn im Wagen heim, <u>damit</u> er nicht nass <u>werde</u>
> er nahm ein Taxi, <u>damit</u> er den Zug nicht <u>versäume</u>

In the colloquial language this use of the special subjunctive is now generally considered stilted. Perhaps the best proof for this is the fact that German students like to use such sentences facetiously—and extensively.

6.123 SPECIAL SUBJUNCTIVE IN SPOKEN GERMAN

Finally, we have to mention the use of the special subjunctive in the spoken language. In modern German, such use is almost completely reserved for cases where the speaker has strong mental reservations about the truth of what he is saying. For example:

> Hans ist nicht mitgekommen, weil er Kopfschmerzen <u>habe</u>
> (but I don't believe he really has a headache)

> Hans ist nicht mitgekommen, weil er Kopfschmerzen <u>hat</u>
> (and I believe it)

> ich habe gelesen, dass Oesterreich Atombomben <u>herstelle</u>
> (but I doubt it)

6.124 SIGNIFICANCE OF SUBJUNCTIVE

Let us repeat in conclusion that the use of the subjunctives generally expresses a mental attitude of the speaker without direct reference to the facts that he conveys. In teaching the subjunctive, we must try to exemplify and define the various appearances of this mental attitude so as to establish a new semantic category in the student's mind.

6.2 PROGRESSIVE FORM

To the layman it may seem odd that the non-existence of a compulsory semantic category in the target language should cause any difficulty, but not to the German teacher who has ever tried to explain the absence of a PROGRESSIVE FORM in German. Our students have very strong and deep-seated grammatical and semantic habits with regard to this form, and it seems inconceivable to them that German does not express the difference between, say,

> what books are you reading?   [and]
> what books do you read?

To the student, the first question is just a casual inquiry, whereas the second one almost amounts to an investigation of character. Thus, he finds it hard to accept that

> was für Bücher lesen Sie?

may mean either one, and only the context or other circumstantial evidence will tell us which English translation is correct. German may, of course, differentiate by some lexical means—but this is not necessary:

> was für Bücher lesen Sie <u>gerade</u>/<u>jetzt</u>?

Other means of expressing the differences between the progressive form and simple verb form have been listed and discussed in §3.1222. Other uses of the -ing m and their equivalents in German have been discussed in §5.241. Here we need only eat once again that the sole remedy for mistakes of the type:

*was für Bücher sind Sie lesend?

nsists of a large number of relevant drills.

6.3 PAST TENSES

In our discussion of compulsory semantic categories, we turn now to a com- rison of the PAST TENSES in our two languages. Since English and German both have past tense (called Modification I in §3.121, e.g. I saw, ich sah) and a present perfect rase (called Modification II in §3.122, e.g. I have seen, ich habe gesehen) our students e always tempted to assume that the difference in meaning between these two forms is e same in both languages. As we all know, this is most decidedly not the case. In Eng- sh the past and the present perfect (or, as some grammarians call them, the simple and e compound past) really do have different meanings; in German, on the other hand, they ffer only stylistically.

6.31 DIFFERENCES IN MEANING OF ENGLISH PAST TENSES

To get at the different meanings in English, let us suppose that you take a trip New York City and that a friend inquires about your sight-seeing there. As long as you e still in New York, the friend will ask: "Have you seen the Statue of Liberty?," using e perfect. But as soon as you come back home, he will ask: "Did you see the Statue of iberty?" using the past. The English present perfect means a segment of time beginning the past but running up to and including the present (in our little story, your trip to New ork). The English simple past tense means a segment of time in the past but not includ- g the present. In English we are forced to talk about past time in either of these two ays, i.e. the difference between the past tenses is a compulsory semantic category in ur native language. An isolated statement like, "Did you (ever) see the Statue of Liberty?" y its very use of the past tense, implies "on some trip which you perhaps took to New ork." And an isolated statement like, "Have you ever seen the Statue of Liberty?" by its ery use of the present perfect, carries the implication "it's still possible for you to see ." Notice that we could no longer use the present perfect if the Statue of Liberty had been estroyed ("*have you seen the Braune Haus in Munich?"); nor would we use it in speaking o a blind man who can no longer see.

This difference in meaning between the English past and perfect is very sub- le and enormously difficult for a foreigner to learn. Quite a few Germans, after having ived in this country for many years, fail to make the correct choice with respect to the ast tenses, though their English may be faultless in other ways.

6.32 DIFFERENCES IN MEANING OF GERMAN PAST TENSES

The difference between the German past tense (ich sah) and present perfect phrase (ich habe gesehen) is a totally different proposition. Using verb forms alone, it i quite impossible in German to make our subtle distinction between chronological past time which does not include the present (I saw) and past time which does include the pr ent (I have seen). A German question like, "Haben Sie die Freiheitsstatue gesehen?" re ly means neither "Have you seen the Statue of Liberty?" (implying that you are still on your trip, that the Statue still exists, and that you still can see) nor "Did you see the Sta ue of Liberty?" (implying that your trip is over, or that the Statue no longer exists, or that you can no longer see). The German question simply refers to past time, and nothin more.

This is to say, the German past tense (ich sah) and present perfect phrase (ich habe gesehen) have exactly the same fundamental denotation: past time. They differ only in stylistic flavor, in their connotation: narrative ich sah, conversational ich habe gesehen. In ordinary conversation, isolated questions and answers about the chronologic past are nearly always in the present perfect phrase. The perfect can also be used in a series of statements: "Erst haben wir uns die Freiheitsstatue angesehen, dann sind wir ins Städtische Kunstmuseum gegangen und schliesslich haben wir die Vereinten Nationen besucht." Said this way, using the perfect phrase, the sentence has a rather lively, vivid style. But the same thing can also be said in the past tense: "Erst sahen wir uns die Fre heitsstatue an, dann gingen wir ins Städtische Kunstmuseum und schliesslich besuchten wir die Vereinten Nationen." Said this way, using the past tense, the three events are strung together into more of a narrative; and this is the narrative style that is always a ways found in expository prose. We can no more translate this difference into English th German can translate the difference between our English past tense and perfect phrase.

In addition to the stylistic differences between the German past tense and the perfect phrase, there exists also a regional difference. The Southern German dialects (i cluding those of Austria and Switzerland) have in the course of their history lost the pas tense: a form corresponding to ich sah simply does not exist in, say, Bavarian. As a con sequence, we find that Southern Germans, as well as Austrians and Swiss, prefer the pr ent perfect even when they are using the standard language. They simply carry over into standard German those speech habits which they first learned in the local dialects. And since in most cases it is the dialect which is their first language, it follows that the use of the past tense (ich sah) is learned only in school where the children are told to emplo these forms in writing compositions. Thus, we find that Southern Germans will use the simple past only on formal occasions, in "official" letters, in essays and reports, etc., whereas in their everyday language, whenever they feel at ease, whenever they want to b friendly, they will use the present perfect. And so we get the strange reaction that the us of the simple past (ich sah) in speaking to "Southerners" immediately casts a chill over the conversation. On the other hand, it is well to mention that Southern Germans, when they speak "hochdeutsch," sometimes tend to overcompensate by using the simple past more frequently than we would expect.

What does all this imply for our classroom situation? We have found that an

:pedient method is to tell the beginners that <u>both</u> the German past <u>and</u> the perfect phrase mean" the past (<u>I saw</u>) in English. Then, as the bewildering array of the irregular German verb forms are being learned, we gradually acquaint the student with those semantic differences which we have described in these paragraphs.

6.33 ENGLISH PRESENT PERFECT AND GERMAN PRESENT TENSE

We have mentioned before (cf. §3.122) that in some instances German will use the present tense where English employs the present perfect phrase. Quite often, but not necessarily, the German sentence will contain the adverb <u>schon</u>. For example:

How long <u>have you been living</u> here?	Wie lange <u>wohnen</u> Sie (schon) hier?
	Seit wann <u>wohnen</u> Sie (schon) hier)
I've <u>been living</u> here for 10 years.	Ich <u>wohne</u> (schon) 10 Jahre hier.
	Ich <u>wohne</u> (schon) seit 10 Jahren hier.

From what we have said above, it follows that if a German said: "Ich habe 10 Jahre hier gewohnt," it would mean 'I lived here for 10 years.'

6.34 CHOICE OF AUXILIARY

One of the problems which our students encounter when forming the present perfect phrase in German is the choice between the auxiliaries <u>haben</u> and <u>sein</u>. Since we have already discussed the semantic categories involving "verbs of motion" and "verbs of inner change" when we described the various verb modifications (cf. §3.12), we need not repeat them here. Note that the most helpful distinction is based on a grammatical category: transitive verbs, i.e. verbs with an object in the accusative case, <u>always</u> form the perfect phrase with the auxiliary <u>haben</u>.

6.35 *LASSEN*

Although we cannot defend it on any grammatical or even semantic grounds, we must include a short discussion of <u>lassen</u> in this paragraph on Past Tenses. The reason is, as every German teacher knows, that our students often fail to distinguish clearly between clauses like

1) I <u>have shined</u> my shoes
2) I <u>have</u> my shoes <u>shined</u>

Students will quickly grasp the difference if we show them that the second (and only the second) clause can be changed to

I'm <u>having</u> my shoes shined   [or]
I <u>have had</u> my shoes shined

When we have thus convinced them that the second clause involves a present tense rather than a present perfect phrase, we can proceed to give them examples involving the various tense forms of <u>lassen</u>.

| 6.4 | MOTION IN REFERENCE TO SPEAKER |

It is difficult to find a handy label for the next compulsory semantic category which we wish to discuss. For want of a better term, let us call it MOTION IN REFERENCE TO THE SPEAKER. In speaking German, we have to make use of this category very frequently, whereas English just barely shows a few traces of it. Let us compare these two sentences:

> he's <u>going</u> home
> he's <u>coming</u> home

The first sentence implies that the person who is spoken about is moving <u>away</u> from the speaker (and, presumably, in the direction home). The second sentence, on the other hand, implies that the speaker is at home and that the person who is spoken about is moving <u>toward</u> the speaker. German shows the same distinction:

> er <u>geht</u> nach Hause   (away from the speaker)
> er <u>kommt</u> nach Hause   (toward the speaker)

In most instances, however, English structure is indifferent as far as motion in reference to the speaker is concerned. Although we usually say "where do you come from?," we hardly ever say "where are you going <u>to</u>?" In fact, quite a large number of English speakers would never use "to," they would always say:

> where are you going?

As a consequence, our beginning students almost invariably say:

> *wo gehen Sie?

Such a question is almost incomprehensible to a German. If it means anything at all, this can only be: 'in what locality do you take a walk?' If "where" is to mean "to what place" German has to say:

> wo gehen Sie <u>hin</u>?
> <u>wohin</u> gehen Sie?

As a result, the student will have to make a choice every time he wants to say "where" in German:

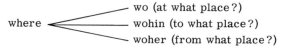

The word <u>her</u> means that the motion described in a sentence is toward the person who is talking ('toward here'). <u>Hin</u> means that the motion is away from the person who is talking ('toward there'). These little words are used very frequently in German. They usually occur with verbs (hinfahren, herfahren), sometimes together with other adverbs (hinaufgehen, heraufgehen). In order to familiarize our students with this semantic category we will have to design drills of this type:

why don't you come down?	kommen Sie doch herunter!
wait, I'm coming down	warten Sie, ich komme hinunter
do come in!	kommen Sie doch herein!
do go in!	gehen Sie doch hinein!
I walked up here	ich bin heraufgegangen
I went up there	ich bin hinaufgegangen, etc.

Later on we may perhaps give our students a list somewhat along these lines:

preposition	adverb	adverb	directional adverbs
aus	aussen	draussen	hinaus / heraus
in	innen	drinnen	hinein / herein
über	-	drüben	hinüber / herüber
unter	unten	drunten	hinunter / herunter
auf	oben	droben	hinauf / herauf

6.41 BRINGEN AND NEHMEN

We should like to end this discussion with a brief remark about bringen and ehmen. In this case the tables are turned: English bring always implies motion toward ıe speaker—German bringen does not carry this implication. German nehmen, on the oth-r hand, almost always implies that something is taken away. Since these verbs are quite requent in use, the number of mistakes our students make is proportionately high. Com-are these examples:

he brought me a pipe	er brachte mir eine Pfeife
bring this book to me	bringen Sie mir das Buch
take this book to him	bringen Sie ihm das Buch
take the book away from him	nehmen Sie ihm das Buch
he took them home	er brachte sie nach Hause (their homes)
he took them home (with him)	er nahm sie (mit) nach Hause (his house)

6.5 NOMINAL GENDER DISTINCTIONS

In our discussion of the grammatical category of GENDER, we mentioned riefly that the most persistent gender indicators in Modern English are not in the nouns hemselves but in the pronouns used to refer to the nouns. That is to say: contrastive airs like king : queen, host : hostess, waiter : waitress are rare. Most of these pairs in

our language tend to disappear, i.e. feminine suffixes are losing ground to the other gen
der indicators. The reason may be that women regard these suffixes as patronizing. A
woman writer wants to be called an author, not an authoress. As a result, many of our s
dents are quite unaware of nominal gender distinctions, and the almost universal (!) gen
der distinctions of German nouns denoting occupation, profession, nationality, etc. const
tute a new compulsory semantic category to them. This semantic category is indeed con
pulsory: the pretty coed stating proudly "ich bin Amerikaner" is considered hilariously
funny by a German. Thus we have to drill this feature of the language. The simplest form
of such a drill would be:

> er ist Lehrer, aber sie ist Lehrerin
> er ist Bäcker, aber sie ist Bäckerin
> er ist Arzt, aber sie ist Ärztin
> er ist Schweizer, aber sie ist Schweizerin
>
> er ist ein Bekannter, aber sie ist eine Bekannte
> er ist der Bräutigam, aber sie ist die Braut

Notice that German does have a few masculine nouns which may stand for persons of either sex: Lehrling, Star, Gast, Liebling. There is also some regional variation. In Germany one would say:

> sie ist Professor an der Universität

but an Austrian says:

> sie ist Professorin an der Universität

But even the Austrian says:

> sie ist Doktor der Philosophie.

6.6 | LOCATION VS. DESTINATION

Because of its very high frequency, the following compulsory semantic category of German is particularly bothersome to the student with an English background:
LOCATION vs. DESTINATION. We have already met one example of this in §6.4:

> where are you staying?   wo übernachten Sie?
> where are you going?   wohin gehen Sie?

Much more frequent, however, are the conflicts caused by this category in the
use of German prepositions. In our classification of German prepositions (cf. §3.51), we
stated that most prepositions govern one and only one case, be it an accusative, a dative,
or a genitive. But there exists a fourth group which governs either an accusative or a dative. This group comprises nine prepositions, all of them having a basic meaning of a "ce
tain spatial relationship": an, auf, hinter, in, neben, über, unter, vor, zwischen. This rela
tionship may be static, denoting a location, or the relationship may be changing, dynamic,
denoting a destination. In the first instance the preposition will govern a dative, in the sec

d instance it will govern an accusative. (Please forgive us for mentioning the following
ther silly mnemonic device, which we include only because it has proved helpful. It is
 tell students that, if the clause answers the question "at what place?" the object of the
eposition will be in the d-at-ive.)

It may be argued that the verb determines the case in which the prepositional
ject appears, since the clause as a whole determines whether the spatial relationship is
atic or dynamic. Thus, it has been said that verbs like sein, bleiben, stehen, liegen, sit-
n will be followed by a preposition + dative, verbs like gehen, stellen, legen, setzen will
 followed by a preposition + accusative. It is true that verbs of the first group most
ten denote locations, verbs of the second group most often destinations. The decisive
ctor, however, remains the question "to what place" vs. "at what place." Contrast for
xample, these two statements:

> er geht hinter das Haus
> er geht hinter dem Haus

ll elements remain equal; the difference between the two clauses is determined only by
e semantic category of destination vs. location. To teach this feature of German we rec-
mmend a large number of contrastive drills of the type:

> er hängt das Bild an die Wand
> das Bild hängt an der Wand
>
> er legt seinen Koffer aufs Bett
> der Koffer liegt auf dem Bett
>
> er geht in den Garten
> er geht im Garten
>
> er stellt den Stuhl vor den Schreibtisch
> der Stuhl steht vor dem Schreibtisch
>
> er fährt seinen Wagen hinter die Schule
> er parkt seinen Wagen hinter der Schule
>
> er hängt ein Foto über das Bett
> das Foto hängt über dem Bett
>
> er stellt einen Papierkorb unter den Tisch
> der Papierkorb steht unter dem Tisch
>
> er stellt das Radio neben sein Bett
> das Radio steht neben seinem Bett
>
> er stellt den Tisch zwischen die Fenster
> der Tisch steht zwischen den Fenstern

The verbs sich setzen, sitzen and sich legen, liegen deserve special attention:

> er setzt sich an die Schreibmaschine
> er sitzt   an der Schreibmaschine

sie <u>legt sich</u> in <u>die</u> Sonne
sie <u>liegt</u>   in <u>der</u> Sonne

sie <u>setzen sich</u> in <u>den</u> Wagen   they're getting into the <u>car</u>
sie <u>sitzen</u>   in <u>den</u> Wagen   they're sitting in the <u>cars</u>

We must keep reminding ourselves and our students that the semantic category of location vs. destination does not affect all prepositions, but only those nine whic we have discussed. Many of the other prepositions also describe spatial relationships, some static, some dynamic. But regardless of the kind of spatial relationship, <u>um</u>, <u>gege</u> etc., always govern the accusative, and <u>zu</u>, <u>nach</u>, <u>aus</u>, etc. always govern the dative. We should point out these inconsistencies to our students lest they be carried away by the s mantic category which we have just described. We must also mention the fact that when these nine prepositions do not refer semantically to spatial relations there is no way of telling what case will be used—though the accusative is more common than the dative. F example:

er wartet auf <u>mich</u>
er macht einen guten Eindruck auf <u>mich</u>

Here the compulsory semantic categories of location and destination simply do not apply We could, of course, tell the students that a German would interpret a dative in these ex amples as meaning "while standing on top of me," but extensive drills are a more lastin solution to this teaching problem.

6.7 | THE SECOND-PERSON PRONOUN

The last semantic category which we wish to describe is not nearly so formi dable as the ones preceding; nevertheless, it causes conflicts and needs to be dealt with. In English we have one 2d person pronoun for singular and plural, for formal and familia relationships, for adults, children, dogs, and suitcases. German, on the other hand, distinguishes three forms:

you ➞ (du ≠ ihr) ≠ Sie

The difference between <u>du</u> and <u>ihr</u> is easily described: <u>du</u> is singular and <u>ihr</u> is plural. The contrast between <u>du/ihr</u> and <u>Sie</u> is more complicated, and there are a few cases where it is hard to say whether to use the familiar or the non-familiar pronoun. Most situations, however, can be unambiguously stated:

<u>du</u> is used in addressing: all children up to about age 14
all animals
all objects, should the occasion arise
all members of the family
a carefully limited number of very close
friends

<u>Sie</u> is used in addressing: all adults who are strangers

all people whom we address with a title re-

gardless how well we know them

The gradual decrease in formality even within the <u>Sie</u>-category can quite eas-
y be described, but it is hard to say when an attempt should be made by the foreigner to
ift from one level to the next. First it is <u>Herr Meyer</u> and <u>Fräulein Müller</u>—next: <u>Herr</u>
obert and <u>Fräulein Luise</u>. Then it is just <u>Robert</u> and <u>Luise</u>, and finally it is <u>Robert</u> and
uise and <u>du</u>.

What should we do in the classroom? We have found it advisable on the senior
gh-school and college levels to ignore the existence of <u>du</u> for a great many lessons, on
e theory that the student needs a lot more German before he is likely to be on such fa-
iliar terms with a German <u>auf deutsch</u> as to have any use for it. (A more important and
rtainly far more practical reason is, of course, that the introduction of <u>du</u> and <u>ihr</u> causes
good many morphological complications which we like to postpone as long as possible.)
grade school and with younger high-school children, we can hardly get away from using
from the very beginning if we wish to retain any semblance of realism in our classroom
scussions and conversations. There we simply have to tell the students that fellow stu-
ents are to be addressed with <u>du</u>, but the teacher and all other adults should be spoken to
s <u>Sie</u>.